T0370327

Poetry
On
Purpose

Devotional Poems

John Richer

WESTBOW
P R E S S®
A DIVISION OF THOMAS NELSON
& ZONDERVAN

WestBow Press books may be ordered through booksellers or by contacting:

WestBow Press
A Division of Thomas Nelson & Zondervan
1663 Liberty Drive
Bloomington, IN 47403
www.westbowpress.com
844-714-3454

ISBN: 978-1-6642-9767-8 (sc)
ISBN: 978-1-6642-9766-1 (e)

Library of Congress Control Number: 2023906867

Print information available on the last page.

WestBow Press rev. date: 06/30/2023

Contents

TWO-YEAR
Devotional Journey with the Lord

My picture in art gallery

This devotional is a way to enjoy poetry and to also spend time looking at themes of the bible. The scripture references in the margin allow you to dig deeper into God's Word for insight and reflection.

These poems were my way to express both the conversations and the questions I had about biblical topics. It was also a personal time of reflection to give extended thought to the things I was personally facing. I shared many of these with my bible study group as I know others face similar issues.

I hope these poems allow you to reflect, ponder and search for God's truth in the Word.

Enjoy,

John.

Remembrance Day

Everywhere I turned to look were signs of what they gave.
Of poppies, graves, and soldier's tears to honor those so brave.
It made me think, *Why does this world just focus on men's war?*
And it made a shiver run through my spine and froze me to my core.

As eyes were watching scenes long past, their memories restored,
I could not help but switch my thoughts to those about my Lord.
While most saw men on ghastly fronts, in fields of dirt and mud,
My mind saw Christ upon the Cross, who shed his precious blood.

Remembrance Day, I know, is meant to honor those who fought
For freedom, peace, and liberty from those whose goals were not.
But no one spoke or thought of Christ, who died upon the cross,
To free us from our captive state; eternal life we'd lost.

We take for granted all he did to take away our sin.
So I give tribute to my God, who now resides within.
And I remember what it took to walk Golgotha's path,
As people turned and spat at him, with faces full of wrath.

Thank God for those who fought so bravely; today we mourn their loss.
But don't forget the One who came and died upon a cross.
Whose blood was shed to save us all, not from one war or two.
Praise Jesus's name, for he is Lord; He died for me and you.

John 3:16

Cross with poppies

He Goes before Us

I thank you, Lord, for blessing me each and every day,
For it is easy to forget you guard and guide my way.
The enemy makes schemes and snares, I often do not see.　　　　(Ps. 142:3)
You have a plan; you go before and spring the traps for me.

My mind can get so full of things; it's hard to learn to walk
The path that you have set for me; that's why you are my rock.　　　　(Ps. 18:2)
You tell me just to look to you for; you will keep me strong.
But still, I let my eyes divert and step to do things wrong.

I thank you that you love me so and wrap me in your arms.　　　　(Deut. 33:27)
You speak each day to guide my soul and set off my alarms,
So I can hear, deep down inside, your words to help me see
The traps and snares that Satan sets to bring much harm to me.

You tell me how I need to fight, and how I can stand strong,
So, I can block the fiery darts and keep my steps from wrong.
I thank you that I can equip the armor you provide,　　　　(Eph. 6:11)
To see the darts as they are thrown, and quickly step aside.

Your shield protects against attacks he sends relentlessly.
You remind me to speak your Word; it is my sword from thee.
You tell me I should thank and praise so I don't start to stray.　　　　(1 Thess. 5:18)
To worship, sing, and dance for you, and always stop to pray.

For when I thank and worship you, and praise you with a shout,
It opens up the world above, and angels you send out.
The mighty host that you control to battle Satan's horde,
And I can smile and know inside that truly, you are Lord.

The helmet you provide for me will help to guard my mind,
And help me run into the fray that I might quickly find.
The words to use to spread good news to all who seek to hear
That Jesus is the King of Kings and conqueror of fear.

My final thoughts I must convey praise and thank you still,
The mighty Lord who stooped to die on top of Calvary's hill.
Your love is great, beyond compare; my words can barely state
The gratitude and awe I feel for making my path straight.   (Isa. 45:2)

Lord of The Valleys

I sat this morning in a haze; my mind could barely cope
As things just spiraled quickly down, like skis upon a slope.
My foe came at my family in ways I did not think,
And for a sec I felt despair and watched my fervor sink.

How fear can grip our hearts so quickly, with words that often sting.
Fear tells us that our path is filled with pain and suffering.
In that brief time I almost choose to think there is no way
That God could make the wrong things right, but then I start to pray.

The fear and worry trouble bring, your Word does quickly smite.
And even in the valley deep, you show your power and might.
And then I hear the words down deep that fortify my heart.
That we are held within your arms, and we've been set apart.

Since health can fail, it reminds me why our faith must be strong.
For in this war that we are in, the battles can be long.
I simply take my fears and doubts and cast them at your feet.
You place a hedge around me still and keep me from defeat.

So even when the mountain's big, I never need to fret.
My prayers and praise set forth your host to cancel out the threat.
I feel your peace that passes all that I can understand.   (Phil. 4:7)
No matter what will happen now, your Word I will command.

A loving dad you truly are, who hears me when I pray.
Who reaches down and comforts me as my thoughts start to stray.
I search your Word; it's always there to help me every day.
It fails me not and guides me well when I don't see a way.   (Ps. 119:105)

How could I not remember all that God has done for me?
He bore my sin, was sacrificed, and died upon a tree.
He conquered sin and rose again, a fact we know is true.   (Rev. 1:18)
He paid the price and stripped from foe his keys of Hades too.

> 1 Kings 20:28 (NKJV)
> Then a man of God came and spoke to the king of Israel, and said, "Thus says the Lord: 'Because the Syrians have said, "The Lord is God of the hills, but He is not God of the valleys," therefore I will deliver all this great multitude into your hand, and you shall know that I am the Lord.'"

The Bible shows us many times how your love never fails.
You free the captive, loose the chains, and open doors to jails.
Yet we forget just whose we are when things don't go our way.
That you are Lord, the King of Kings, and have the final say.

You send us out into the world equipped to fight each day,
But only if we read your Word and follow what you say.
You stay with us; you never leave, no matter where we are.
No mountaintop or valley floor, no distance is too far.

(Luke 9:1)

A Revelation Story

I closed my eyes to pray and dwell and think about my Lord.
Of all the times his love has flowed, and onto me it poured.
I thanked the Lord for all he's done, all his great provision,
Yet God was asking if I would receive a different vision.

I always think of God as love; it's how I picture him.
But God was leading me to see my view was way too slim.
So as I closed my eyes and said, "Lord, show me what you will,"
A vivid scene was set for me upon a distant hill.

I heard a noise and cupped my eyes, strained to look up higher.
I saw a man upon a horse, eyes like flames of fire.   (Rev. 1:14)
His hair was wool, as white as snow; his sash was bright gold.
His feet were like a bronze sculpture fresh from a fiery mold.

And as he spoke, I clasped my ears; it boomed like thunder's peal.
His face a sun so dazzling bright, I fought the urge to kneel.
My eyes could hardly look at him, brilliant was his glory.
I remembered words I'd read, a Revelation story.

The angels stood upon a field, watched as he descended.
As heaven's host looked to their king, swords and shields extended.
I watched them charge at Satan's troops, battles quickly finished,
For Satan's horde stood badly scored, numbers much diminished.

Somehow I thought the battle would be on a grander scale.
Then suddenly it dawned on me that Satan had to fail.
For God knows all, he had control, it never was in doubt.   (1 John 3:20)
Yet Satan's lies had covered up God's victory and rout.

It made me think of how I thought I had to fight a foe
That had a chance of beating me, but it was all a show.
His tricks and schemes were all he had, yet still I feared his might.   (Eph. 6:11)
I shook my head and realized then my thoughts had not been right.

For Christ had won the war before I even had been born.
He conquered sin and death for me; the temple veil was torn.   (Matt. 27:51)
To signify his mighty deed, the angels cheered with glee.
And now I know his victory had paid the price for me.

The scene was fading from my eyes, and suddenly I woke.
It finally now had dawned on me that Satan's lies were smoke.
A risen Lord, a battle won were what I had to see.
So anytime I called his name, I claimed my victory.

For when you let Christ in your heart, it's more than just rebirth.
For greater is my God within than he who holds this earth.   (1 John 4:4)
His promises will not fail me, no matter what life brings.
He reigns on earth and heaven too; He is the King of Kings.

And Satan's troops, who fear his name, tremble at his power.
For they know that when he returns, they'll see their final hour.
Against the foes, he wields his might, and so the story ends
When captured beast and false prophet into the lake he sends.   (Rev. 1:19, 20)

But I go to my father's house, which he prepares for me,   (John 14:2)
And join the saved in worship songs for all eternity.
Even though this chapter ends, there's more to this story.
For I will live eternally, with God and all his glory.

Soldier with shield with cross on it

Poem Journal: God's Inspiration:

WEEK 5

Sticks and Stones

Though sticks and stones could break my bones, names would never hurt me.
When as a child I heard those lines, I thought they were trustworthy.
Yet as I look at youth today, so stressed, and full of fear,
I realize now those lies had caused depression to appear.

So when I search the Word of God, I start to see the truth,
That words do hurt and badly scar the feelings of our youth.
So many kids are sad today, and others are confused,
Because we have as parents failed to watch the words we've used.

Their self-esteem and self-worth shrink as cruel words knock them down.
Since we have not prepared them well, mentally they drown.
So parents, I reach out to you with guidance I have found.
For in God's Word there are some tips to make your counsel sound.

It says in Psalms that all our kids are gifts from God on high. (Ps. 127:3)
So cherish them and give them hope so their dreams start to fly.
Teach that when they obey you, it's doing what God asks. (Col. 3:20)
Plus doing so will please the Lord, who guides them in their tasks.

And let them know it is God's will for them to grow up wise.
The secret is the Word of God, which puts down Satan's lies.
For his Word helps to guard their minds, so Satan can't condemn,
It helps them reach their destiny, which God has planned for them.

And then they can be ready for whatever life will bring,
And live a life that pleases God and helps their hearts to sing.
Then they will know that God made them; each one his hands did make. (Ps. 139:13, 14)
For God himself decreed their birth, not one was a mistake.

So when they err or break the rules, be there to set them straight.
For discipline shows that we care if done in love, not hate. (Prov. 13:4)
For God's own Word confirms this fact: We must teach them some rules.
For parents who will not do this raise children to be fools.

Help raise them up and make them strong; guide them with instruction. (Prov. 1:8, 9)
Then they can walk a path that will help avoid destruction.
When more than sticks or stones are thrown, it will no longer scar,
For self-esteem and self-worth come when they know whose they are.

For we all want our children to grow mighty in the Lord,
To seek his face and search his Word, his promises to hoard.
And when they feel their thoughts attacked, the Word of God appears.
It is a shield, a victor's crown to fight off any fears. (Rev. 3:11)

So think about the words you choose, the power punch they pack.
For words do hurt, as I've found out, once sent, you can't get back.
So if you heed God's Word in this, you'll see a fire lit.
For when they train in what is right, they will remember it. (Prov. 22:6)

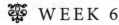
Name above All Names

At church today I realized how his Word speaks to our hearts.
It's not the way some folks may think; we all hear different parts.
His Word showed me his attributes, his name above all names.[1]   ([1]Phil. 2:9)
So I looked up; I had to see, just what the Bible claims.

Today I saw some of his names the scriptures had for him.
The ones you often read or sing in Bible verse or hymn.
I realized then so many things his titles did confer,
Like "Prince of Peace"[2] and "Mighty God"[3] and "Blessed Redeemer."[4]   ([2,3]Isa. 9:6; [4]Prov. 23:11)

The "Holy One,"[5] the "Son of God,"[6] the "Bright and Morning Star."[7]   ([5]Isa. 54:5; [6]Dan. 3:25; [7]Rev. 22:16)
So many ways, oh Lord I see, just who you truly are.
"Emmanuel,"[8] he goes with us, "the truth, the life, the Way."[9]   ([8]Isa. 7:14; [9]John 14:6)
The "Good Shepherd"[10] who tends his flock, protecting ones who stray.   ([10]John 10:11)

For God so loved, the Bible says, he sent his Son to be
An "offering,"[11] the "Lamb of God,"[12] the "ransom"[13] paid for me.   ([11]Eph. 5:2; [12]John 1:29; [13]Matt. 20:28)
Nailed to a cross, the "sacrifice,"[14] in full our debt he paid,   ([14]Heb. 13:15)
Though scourged and mocked and crucified, a "sure foundation"[15] laid.   ([15]Isa. 28:16)

So wonderful[16] our "counselor"[17] that he can plead our case.   ([16,17]Isa. 9:6)
The "advocate"[18] who mediates, his blood stands in our place.   ([18]Isa. 9:6)
He's at God's side, the great "High Priest,"[19] so we are freed from sin,   ([19]Heb. 4:14)
And I can cling to the "true vine"[20] and change my heart within.   ([20]John 15:1)

For he is crowned with many crowns;[21] We know him as "Messiah,"[22]   ([21]Rev. 19:12; [22]Dan. 9:25, 26)
"Chief Corner Stone,"[23] the "Living Bread,"[24] and even "Lion of Judah."[25]   ([23]Eph. 2:20; [24]John 6:51; [25]Rev. 5:5)
Some terms we know, and some may be new; he is the "Light and Glory,"[26]   ([26]Luke 2:32)
But each is told to let us know there's more to his story.

My "saviour"[27] lives, the "Word made Flesh,"[28] too many names to tally.   ([27]John 4:42; [28]John 1:14)
Above the rest, without compare, the "Lily of the valley."[29]   ([29]Song of Sol. 2:1)
"Rose of Sharon,"[30] pure and true, one we can depend on.   ([30]Song of Sol. 2:1)
He came to make our lives complete, the "Rock"[31] which we can lean on.   ([31]1 Cor. 10:4)

The "Alpha"[32] and the "Omega,"[33] from start until the end.   ([32, 33]Rev. 1:11)
He's "King of Kings"[34] and "Lord of Lords,[35] and on my knee I bend.   ([34, 35]1 Titus 6:15)
Now we can praise, and use his name; it comes with power and might
To heal the sick, cause lame to walk, and blind men to gain sight.

I stand in awe since no one else can claim what Jesus claims.
Faithful and true he is to us, the "Name above all Names."   ([36]Rev. 3:14)
There is no one to challenge him, who dares defy my Lord.
And you can see all who he is; his might can't be ignored.

Mercy Follows Me

We hear of wrath, we hear of might, but God is more than that.
His love is great, exceeding all, and never will fall flat.
We know that love can conquer all, but why is that so true?
Because he shows that mercy is his gift to me and you.

So what does mercy mean to me, and what does it entail?
It is how God pours out his love when we begin to fail.
And sure, he sits upon a throne, and righteousness he wears,
But mercy he bestows on us to show he truly cares.

His mercy is more than a word; it's actions he has made.
His blood was spilt upon a cross so judgment could be stayed.
For only he could pay this debt; he knew this was his path,
So he could show the world below that mercy outweighed wrath.

In the old books, we heard men plead, "Have mercy on me, Lord,"
Because they knew that God above was not to be ignored.
The wages of our sin is death, so how could we atone?   (Rom. 6:23)
A spotless lamb would die for us, and pay the price alone.

So God planned out through mercy's eyes just how we could achieve
The fee of death, that we owed him, by sending our reprieve.
This Christmastime we celebrate how Jesus came to earth.
The greater gift he gave to us was dying, not his birth.

For when he died, his mercy showed how much he loved us all.   (John 3:16)
For he so loved, he sent his Son, so Satan's reign could fall.
I bow my knee, just like the saints who perished long ago,
And praise his name for I now know his mercy he will show.   (Ps. 86:5)

His mercy now I always trust to keep me safe from harm.   (Ps. 13:5)
It covers me and will not flee; I wear it like a charm.   (Ps. 66:20)
To the throne of grace I boldly come whenever I'm in need.   (Heb. 4:16)
For I know that the Lord loves me; his mercy will succeed.

I thank you, Lord, that mercy is what brought me back to you,
When I was lost and rambled on and wandered with no clue.
Your grace I see, extended thus, with mercy as its source.
So when I fall, you pick me up and help me find my course.

I now can see that mercy is more than forgiving sin.
It is your core, just who you are, a force that is within.
It seeks us out when we did not deserve a gift at all.
It finds the lost and gives them hope and helps them to stand tall.

It seeks to go places where no person wants to be,
To let the worst of sinners know that your love is the key.
That all have failed, and Jesus came to set the captives free.
That mercy is his way to help, so guilt cannot hold thee.

Perfect Peace

The world, to me, goes rushing by; it's hard to see it all.
And when God speaks in his still small voice, I strain to hear his call.
I finally found the perfect way to take things day by day.
God beckons me to rest awhile and listen when I pray.   (Exod. 33:14)

The key to life is to seek ye first the kingdom of the Lord,   (Matt. 6:33)
And he can help you navigate as long as he's onboard.
For from the Lord come peace and hope to help those gone astray,
For God will not forsake nor leave, he promises to stay.   (1 Chron. 28:20)

He leaves with me a perfect peace, a peace without compare.   (Isa. 26:3)
For peace can help us to relax, when life's pace leaves us bare.
Peace is the cloak that God gives us, a blessing to us all,   (Ps. 29:11)
With righteousness, when both combined, we won't be prone to fall.   (Isa. 32:17)

He is the source of peacefulness; we can't find it alone.   (Jer. 8:15)
For those who fail to heed God's Word, his peace will not be known.   (Ezek. 7:25)
For they don't see that stress and fear are from the one who lies.   (1 Cor. 14:33)
As they seek things to bring them peace, false dreams they idolize.

It says his peace should follow you, and from your mouth should flow,
To be a gift, you bring to those in places you would go.   (Luke 10:5)
For if we bring both peace and joy, the world cannot resist,
For in them is a longing for these things their lives have missed.

The kingdom is not meat and drink but righteousness and peace,   (Rom. 14:17)
Which gives joy in the Holy Ghost, who helps our stress decrease.
Since only God has full control, with peace he calmed the sea.   (Mark 4:39)
It just makes sense to honor him, and peace he'll give to thee.

Since God is peace so glorious, it's tough to understand   (Phil. 4:7)
How big a role it is for us when it's at our command.
So God, we thank you with all our hearts for this gift that you gave those
Who seek your face and worship you; your kingdom they have chose.

Praise be to God, the Prince of Peace, for choosing to give me
This gift of peace, which when I seek, will fill my life with glee.   (1 Pet. 3:11)
I wrap this up—one final thought—is that I got this free.
And as I learn about my Lord, it multiplies for me.   (2 Pet. 1:2)

Every Knee Shall Bow

I often think and ponder if my life is like the rest.
I laugh, I cry, I go to work; I try to be my best.
But God tells me I'm set apart; he consecrates my life,   (Lev. 20:7)
While all around I see a world that's full of hate and strife.

He offers life to everyone if they will only start
To hear his voice and quiet knock, and let him in their heart.   (Rev. 3:20)
Some people think they have a choice, but one day they will see
that in the end, he's King of Kings; he rules eternity.

The world goes on without regard for God who made it all.
And scoff and sneer at those who choose to heed and trust his call.
So many choose to walk away, their inner core still chilled,
For they know not what he can do to make their lives fulfilled.

A time will come when he will not be laughed at or ignored.
For every knee and every tongue will prove that he is Lord.   (Rom. 14:11)
So better to be on his side then forced to praise his name.
Be king or queen, be rich or poor, your fate will be the same.

For in God's Word it clearly states that every knee will bend,
So those that mock and dismiss God will see that mindset end.   (Luke 18:32)
A time will come when every man from his tongue will confess
That Jesus Christ is Lord of Lords, no matter their address.

I thank the Lord that he saved me, and I can call him Lord,
For he has made my life complete, and his blessings I will hoard.
And one day soon I'll be with him and gladly bow my knee.
And he will lift me up and say, "My blood has set you free."   (Rom. 6:18)

And I will be part of those who see this all unfold,
As all the earth bows to his name, and speaks those words so bold.
That Jesus Christ is Lord of Lords, and King of all the earth.
The risen Lord, the Son of God, the pearl of greatest worth.   (Matt. 13:46)

Longing for My Lord

I heard in church and often sang a song about a deer.
My mum would hum or sing its tune, and I would stop to hear.
It told a tale of how it pants and looks to find a source   (Ps. 42:1)
Of water, which it can partake and quench its thirst in course.

And then I found that like the deer, my soul begins to long   (Ps. 63:1)
To seek the Lord and know his will, like I heard in the song.
I never thought, at that young age, that I would feel this way.
But as I learned about my God, I felt it every day.

And even when I turned away and followed my own path,
It wasn't long before my soul began to do the math.
It told me how, no matter what, my God was always there,   (Heb. 13:5)
And how my life could be much more if I would only dare.

No matter what I chose to do, I always felt within
A need to praise and worship him, so my soul could drink in.
The needed life he did provide for all who sought his face.
For only God did my soul search; I longed for his embrace.

The song went on to tell me how he was my strength and shield.   (Ps. 18:2)
And when I chose to put him first, my spirit then could yield.
How I could find the joy he gives to all who call him Lord.
He's more than gold and silver too; he is the best reward.

It's hard to put in rhyming words how deep my feelings went.
The longing grew; still wanting more, my thirst would not relent.   (Matt. 5:6)
For as I kept on learning more about how much God loved me,
Still deeper yet, my longing went, like roots under a tree.

So many yearn for this closeness, too, yet choose to walk away.   (Job 21:14)
Their hearts are cold to God's desire; their lives have gone astray.
But if we stop and humbly yield, our lives he can repair   (Ps. 10:17)
And teach our souls to long for him and save us from despair.

So like a deer, I'm thirsty for the water he can bring.
My soul cries out, "You are my God," and makes me want to sing
That he's my friend and closer still than anyone could be.   (Prov. 18:24)
So that is why I long for him: He is my destiny.

God, Why Not Me?

I tend to sit and look around and hear what others say
Of blessings they have gotten from God, while mine seem far away.
I want to sing and shout for joy, and see his blessings flow.
But daily life has stressed me out; I haven't seen them show.

I know that I cannot compare my life to those around.   (Heb. 12:1)
Yet lack and pain seem my allies, and struggles do abound.
One question stirs that saddens me, which makes my day get worse:
Why do some thrive, their wallets full, yet empty is my purse?

And then he says my life is like the four seasons of a year.
I'm like a tree that needs them all before the fruit appears.
The spring shows growth, but autumn lacks, as loss seem to take root.
But God's got this; he prunes and trims so I can bear some fruit.   (Ps. 1:3)

But don't seek wealth or covet things; just seek his kingdom first.   (Matt. 6:33)
Then all these things he promises will surely be dispersed.
So I must put my faith in him; he said what he would do—   (Matt. 6: 30–34)
That he will bless and bring me joy, his promise would come true.

For God is King and loves me so; his Word he'll always keep.
For soon I will look back at this and realize I thought cheap.
For in his Word he tells me that my faith and trust are key.   (James 1:6)
He sees what is and guards my path, my future's planned for me.

So stay in faith as others pray to make your dreams unfold.   (Rom. 12:3; 2 Tim. 1:13)
But even when they do appear, remember God's our gold.
The best reward that we can get is finding his embrace,
For blessings here mean nothing soon, when we will see his face.

.

The key in this is to stay in faith when blessings seem to hide.
No matter what we struggle through, he's always at our side.   (Heb. 13:5)
So when it seems that things look dim, and his gifts seem so late,
He knows our path and how it's bent, and then makes the crooked straight.

So praise his name; do not despair, no matter what comes near.
He holds you in his arms with care, so you never need to fear. (Deut. 33:27)
God goes with you if you will choose to seek his will each day.
He is the God who walks with us; he never goes away.

One final thought I leave with you to strengthen your resolve.
As you walk close, his favor grows, and problems will dissolve. (Ps. 5:12)
He loves justice and all his saints; they are his one true love. (Ps. 33:5)
The faithful ones, he says abound in blessings from above. (Prov. 28:20)

The Earth Cries Out

I often think about how we are made in the image of our God.
And how we have a soul within, which always seeks his nod.
But not just we, creation too, knows that he is their King.
And in the Word we see it says that all the earth can sing.

We know that God can use it all to make his will unfold.
He used a whale, a donkey too when prophets got too bold. (John 1:17; Num. 22: 21–33)
When donkeys talk and whales spit out the people who resist, (Num. 22:28; John 2:10)
It proves to all that everything, without him can't exist.

He parts the seas and opens earth to swallow up the cursed. (Num. 16:32)
And from a rock makes water flow to quench his children's thirst.
We see him do some mighty deeds to prove he has a plan.
For what is there, he cannot do, creation proves he can.

The trees sing out for him to come and clap for all to hear. (1 Chron. 16:33)
And fields cry out a joyful noise, and mountains sing with cheer. (Isa. 55:12)
He made it all—the rocks and trees, the hills and valleys too.
They listen with inclined ear to hear his words so true. (Deut. 32:1)

This is the day the Lord has made, from morning to the night.
So I rejoice and remain glad, and worship with delight.
I join the earth to praise his name, with hands held in the air,
For only God could make a world with so much love and care.

Remember well the scriptures' signs of what our Lord can do
If you do not accept his call, or let the Lord guide you.
For all creation heeds the Lord, and at his word will shout.
And even if we held our peace, the stones would soon cry out. (Luke 19:40)

For heaven stands beside the earth to witness all he is. (Deut. 4:26)
So follow him—do not resist—and let your voice join his.
Since he can use a storm or rain to make his people know
That he, as God, controls it all, above and down below.

So sing a song unto the Lord, and praise his name on high.
For everywhere, the earth cries out, from ocean to the sky.
There is no doubt he is the Lord of everything there is.
For we are not the only ones that recognize we're his.

Changing Channels

We all go through tough times in life, some small and some immense.
And even when it looks too much, through God, it can make sense.
We often find the problem lies within and not without.
Our mind begins to play its game, a coaster ride of doubt.

We start to see what can go wrong, as though it has come true.
The movie starts within our brain, and visions cloud our view.
We see ourselves begin to fail and watch our world collapse.
But this is how he keeps us blind; it's one of Satan's traps.

We see ourselves as weak and old, or failures all alone.
These scenes can cause us to lose hope and turn our will to stone.
But these are lies to keep us bound, so we don't see the facts
That God loves us and has a plan, so we can foil attacks.

The first step is to guard our mind, so we can win the race,   (Deut. 4:9)
We are his kids and do possess his blessings and his grace.
When Satan lies, we must push back with promises God gives.
The first of which he sent his Son, who died, but now he lives.   (2 Cor. 13:4)

An advocate, our coach and guide, he never leaves our side.   (Job 16:19)
So we should never feel alone, it was for me he died.
Our sins are paid, the debt is gone, a wretch I am no more.   (1 Cor. 15:3)
And when my worth is questioned, I quickly close the door.

My mind must change the channel that the enemy has chosen.
Instead, I pick another one, where Jesus Christ had arose.
I am a new creation now; I will not let those lies
Keep me depressed and powerless, no matter how he tries.

His fear and gloom I will replace with faith and joy and hope.
The channel stays on one I choose and helps my mind to cope.
The words he used to hold my mind no longer keep me down.
I read God's Word, which makes me strong, so he can't steal my crown.   (2 Titus 1:7)

A worthless one becomes God's child; my value has increased.
"You'll die alone," turns to God's home, where there will be a feast.
"God can't love you," is changed to "My God loves me so much."
"You can't get well," is simply gone; I see his healing touch.

Your sin is bad, forgiveness trumps, his Son has paid my bail.
Evil reigns are countered with, "My God will never fail."
"Life's just too hard," is beaten by, "He will not let me fall."
"Your faith is weak," is blocked by truth, "In Christ I can do all."   (Phil. 4:13)

The key to these—like all his lies—is knowing God's got this.
And he goes with us everywhere, so Satan's arrows miss.
So now I have a channel on that always shows he can,
So long as I have faith in God and trust he has a plan.

The Unseen Realm

We strive to know what we did wrong when our prayers seem unheard.
Did we show doubt or not live up to our role in the Word?
We hear it said it is our faith that dictates how things go.
So did we fail to ask God's will, or did God fail to show?

It can deflate and make us think that faith is hit or miss.
But there is more than just our prayers that play a role in this.
For no one knows what God has planned since he controls it all.
And we must trust he has a plan and did not drop the ball.

The Bible says when Daniel prayed, God heard his prayers on high.
And we would think with this man's faith, he'd soon see God's reply.
An angel left to bring God's Word but found his pathway blocked   (Dan. 10:12–14)
For Satan had God's angel stopped; I read this and was shocked.

So God sent more to help break through the troops who blocked his way.
Instead of quick, it took some time—three weeks, just not one day.
I realize now there's always more than just the world we see.
The heavenly realm is also real and has an impact on me.

I know that God is in control, but we need to accept
That Satan has some forces, too, and wants to intercept.
The blessings and the help our God has planned for me and you,
Our words and thoughts can sometimes help make room for Satan's crew.

He lies to us and gets us to support him in his scheme.
So guard your mind and armor up, so his troops can't gain steam.
We know that he, from Eden's fall, has sought to deceive man.
But in the end, he cannot win; God always has a plan.

So when you pray, it's safe to say, the adversary tries
To counteract and shake your faith with whispers and more lies.
To truth be told when Jesus died, he crippled Satan's might.
He took the keys that Satan held so death had lost its bite.   (Rev. 1:18)

But there are some who do not think that angels do exist,
That Hades won't become our fate if God's will we resist.
Our foe has spun so many views that most are unaware
That Satan has demonic hordes that try to block our prayer.

But Jesus is the King of Kings, dominion he controls.
But even though the devil lost, he seeks to capture souls.
He lies and tells us constantly that we deserve much less
Than what our Lord has promised us and what we can possess.

So be prepared to get attacked when you seek first our Lord.
But if you stand upon the Rock, your faith will be restored.
We battle not with flesh and blood but Satan's forces too.   (Eph. 6:12)
So meditate upon his Word, and your mind it will renew.   (1 Pet. 1:13; Rom. 12:2)

Heart of a King

The book of Psalms I like to read; it comes from David's heart.
From early on we see his life, where he was set apart.
We see how God prepared him for the role he'd one day play.
But long before he took the throne, he learned to praise and pray.

He started in a lowly spot while tending Jesse's flocks.   (1 Sam. 17:15)
But here is where he forged his strength and learned to sling his rocks.
It's often said that David had a heart that sought the Lord
For David chose to seek him first, before he held a sword.

His brothers were the mighty ones, who people saw as great.
And David was, to many folks, the least of Jesse's eight.   (1 Sam. 17:12)
God saw a man whose heart was pure and worthy to be king.
And that is why the oil did flow; anointing it did bring.

It goes to show how our God works in different ways than we,
Who tend to judge by outside looks and not one's pedigree.
But God sees through the fake facades and sees what's in our heart.
He sees when we seek our own way and think that we are smart.

When David faced the Philistine, he knew he would prevail.
Because his God was beside him, he simply could not fail.
He looked not at the giant's might but focused on his Lord.
He saw a man and ran at him, and never brought a sword.

This tale is told by many folks as beating all the odds.
But it is not about his skill; it showcased only God's.
God is the One who prepared him to reach his destiny.
And it shows how, when we serve God, he gives us victory.

For David sought to serve his king, the mighty one called Saul.
Whom God had placed upon the throne but let his kingdom fall.
When jealousy and foolish pride made Saul feel paranoid,
It made his heart grow dark and cold as evil filled the void.

The ladies sang that Saul had killed a thousand of his foes,
But David killed ten thousand men; it's how their ballad goes.
So Saul did plot to end the threat he felt would take his throne.
And tried to kill him many times; his hate was now full blown.

But through it all, we can see how God worked in David's life
And taught him to depend on him through conflict and the strife.
The things I learn from reading this are traits that he displayed,
The times he praised and thanked the Lord while he was most afraid.

For when he thought he would be killed, God proved to be his ward,
Which turned the fear and doubt he had to trust in the Lord.
He often cried to God above to hark and give his ear.
I often think how bold he was to call his God so near.

He asked his God to save him from all those who sought his death.
Yet often when we feel alone, we fail to use our breath.
When David asked, he knew inside that God would hear his plea,
And if his foes prepared a trap, his God would set him free.

I wrap this up with one last thought about how David prayed.
He asked his God for everything and never was afraid.
He asked his God to keep him safe whenever things went bad.
And I should do like David did as God also is my dad.

Wisdom Calls

I had an urge to try to find why wisdom was sought out.
I always liked when Proverbs told how wisdom seemed to shout.   (Prov. 1:20)
Why was it so, why need to shout for wasn't it a prize?   (Job 28:18; Prov. 8:11)
Yet time and time, the Bible showed how fools sought Satan's lies.

They shunned the thing that could help them bring joy into their life
And chose to seek their folly first, which brought in pain and strife.   (Prov. 13:10)
For wisdom cries at our heart's gate and begs to let her stay,   (Prov. 8:1)
For when a man lets wisdom in, it is a joyous day.   (Prov. 3:13)

Wisdom protects just like a shield and defends against our foes.   (Prov. 2:7)
Incline your ear to hear her call for from our God she flows.   (Prov. 2:2, 6)
For when she lives within your heart, true happiness will reign.   (Prov. 3:13)
Understanding and good advice are fruits that you will gain.   (Prov. 13:10; 2:2)

So how do I receive this thing that many fail to find?
It starts with what the Bible says since I, myself, am blind.
Fear of the Lord is how it starts; I must seek first my Lord.   (Job 28:28)
A hidden pearl he gives to me; my heart is where it's stored.   (Col. 2:3; Prov. 14:33)

And once I have discovered it, my life will start to bloom.
Wisdom brings hope and peace to me, while foolish men seek doom.   (Prov. 24:14; 1 Kings 5:12)
For lacking it can lead to pain for folly leads astray.   (Prov. 10:21)
But wisdom gives discretion to and helps to guide our way.   (Prov. 3:21)

Wisdom is pure and gentle, too, and always helps another.   (James 3:17)
It surely comes from God above, faithful like a brother.
It stays with us but blesses all, makes understanding kin.   (Prov. 7:4)
Pay attention to its voice, and heed its direction.   (Prov. 5:1)

It is the thing I seek the most to guide my daily walk.   (Eccles 10:10)
Especially since the world we're in can only hate and mock.
All that our Lord has done for them, yet still, he won't let go.
So give me strength and wisdom too; speak seeds that God can sow.

For Wisdom is a part of you; it helped create the earth   (Prov. 3:19)

When you spoke forth and formed it all, when life was at its birth.   (Jer. 10:12)

It builds a house where all can stay and calls to all who hear.   (Prov. 9:1)

And I, for one, will listen well and to its words adhere.

Fear and Paranoia

We look around the world today; it's full of fear and doubt.
As panic starts with people sick, a virus did break out.
And as it spreads, the fear becomes more deadly than the cause.
As people feel it hit their lives, despair sharpens its claws.

As people fight and run amok, their actions based in fear,
As every day more folks get sick, its presence is drawing near.
Our way of life—our family's too—seems closer to this risk
As paranoia, fear, and doubt stir trouble like a whisk.

It's easy to see how this starts for people fear disease.
So anxiousness and worry lurk; life has no guarantees.
Yet why am I not feeling so, what makes me feel at rest?
It is because I trust my God, who wants for me the best.   (Matt. 7:11)

We realize that our hope is placed on him and him alone.   (Ps. 31:24)
So fear cannot attach itself; He is my cornerstone.   (Ps. 118:22)
I realize that I do not know what road will lie ahead.
But I will praise him all day long, no matter what is said.   (Ps. 71:14)

The news cannot break through my wall; he shields me from this fear.
He guides me through no matter what may happen or appear.
It also lets me tell the world God reigns and has control.   (Dan. 2:21)
And whether I get sick or not, His name I will extol.

For in the end, it matters not, eternal life is mine.   (John 3:15)
So let the storm rage 'round my house, my family will be fine.
God uses things for his glory; I do not know just how.   (Rom. 9:23)
But I trust him to see me through; I'll praise him anyhow.

So do not fear in what you see or read or even hear.
For God knows all and gives to us the peace that conquers fear.   (John 14:27)
The pain I feel is not for me but for those lost in this time.
For dread and fright are all they know as worry starts to climb.

But we as those God set apart must use this as a chance
To show them Christ, who conquered death and stymies fear's advance.
For if they cling upon the Rock, the storms will not feel fierce.   (Matt. 7: 24, 25; Luke 6:48)
Paranoia can't come in; his shield it cannot pierce.

So what makes us impervious when fear and panic rise?
We know that this is not our home, it's not our final prize.   (1 Chron. 29:15)
For Jesus went, prepared a place, our heavenly landlord,   (John 14:2)
So all who serve him as their Lord, their hope will be restored.   (Zech. 9:12)

Where there is hope, despair must flee; with peace there is no fear.
Paranoia cannot exist with truth and wisdom near.
God has these gifts, they come from him, they serve to light our way.
And even when things seem so grim, fearfulness cannot stay.

Tell everyone that God's got this; he has the final say.
He loves us so and cares for us, and guards us day to day.
So praise his name in all these things; fear's grip has lost its hold,   (Ps. 42:11)
And though the world is full of dread, my hope will stand up bold.

Trust in the Lord

I often find, when holding fast, my faith must be renewed.
For when I stand in faith awhile, my hope can come unglued.
I wonder why this happens when I started out so strong.
I prayed, believed, and spoke his Word, what could have gone so wrong?

It is because I do not know just when the Lord will act.
So I must keep my faith held strong; I need my hope intact.
So how do I renew my strength when I grow tired and weak?
The secret lies in God's own Word, the answers I must seek.

Isaiah said to regain strength, we wait upon the Lord.   (Isa. 40:31)
It's God who gives us energy if we're in one accord.
He gives us might and increases power so our strength does not wane.   (Isa. 40:29)
His joy can help rejuvenate when hope begins to drain.

The Word tells us that we can rise with wings like eagles too.   (Isa. 40:31)
This illustrates how God lifts us, so we can make it through.
It's Jesus who can give us this, like water in dry land.   (Isa. 32:2)
For he cannot become weary, he sits at God's right hand.   (Isa. 40:28)

Remember what he did for us, the price his body paid.
Consider what he suffered through, and you won't be dismayed.   (Heb. 12:3)
So stand, be brave, be strong, endure; this is his wish for us.   (1 Cor. 16:13)
Like Job, who would not curse his God, he uttered not one cuss.   (Job 2:9)

He is a shield, and he knows best; his Word is proven right,   (Ps. 18:30)
A stronghold where I can find rest when trouble is in sight.   (Nah. 1:7; Ps. 91:2)
He heeds my prayers if I trust him; the Bible tells me so.   (1 Chron. 5:20)
So when I feel the pressure mount, into his arms I go.

There is no man who can compare, so keep your trust in God.   (Ps. 118:8–9)
Don't let your mind deter your faith, our thinking can be flawed.   (Prov. 3:5)
No worldly might, no force on earth, will be what I trust in.   (Ps. 20:7)
For only God can save our soul and forgive us our sin.   (1 Tim 4:10)

So when I feel like giving up, my courage will not bend.   (Heb 10:23)
And I shall gain the confidence I need until the end.
His promises he's sure to keep; he's faithful, and he's true.   (Rev. 19:11)
So keep hope strong and don't let go; he will deliver you.   (Job 27:6)

Patience Tested

I want to try to be my best when things around me swirl.
There are lots of things that will help me: How do I find that pearl?
I know of faith and hope and peace, quite mighty are those three.
But one that I forget to use waits patiently for me.

For patience is the biggest thing; without it, hope recedes.   (Rom. 15:4)
And doubt will start to creep right in, and then my faith concedes.
Then peace is left bereft of hope and drains from me so quick.
For I had failed to be patient and trust his plan to click.

God's timing is at his command; he chooses how and when.
I simply have to let it go and trust it's now or then.
Patience helps us to hold on tight when we don't see his plan.
It is what helps us grow in him; it profits every man.   (James 1:4)

Patience comes from God above; forgiveness is its trait.
He watches us as we fall down but helps our path turn straight.
Patience of Christ should be our goal, endurance to the end.   (2 Thess. 3:5)
Then we can gain maturity, so our faith will not bend.   (2 Thess. 1:4)

For when we face chaos and trials, his power will sustain.   (Col. 1:11)
Experience and long-suffering will help our faith remain.
Love is patient, hope is as well; it's why he waits and knocks.
And if you let him rule your life, much patience he unlocks.

So as you see, they all fit well—faith, patience, peace, and hope.
But patience is the glue that binds and helps our minds to cope.
So be patient, trust in the Lord, let patience work for you,   (James 1:3)
And in the end, you'll be complete, whatever you go through.   (James 1:4)

It teaches us another thing, why God's love will prevail.
For patience is his strongest trait, no matter how we fail.
So worry not when trials invade; it is as God has planned.
He's using them to work on you, so your life will be grand.

So since it is one of his traits, we should pursue it too.   (1 Tim. 6:11)

And when it's used on other folks, we mirror his virtue.   (Rom 15:5)

To forgive those who mistreat us should always be our goal.

Cling to patience—it's needed most—it will help win your soul.   (Luke 21:19)

Praise Unleashed

I looked at the psalms and realized how often they mentioned praise,
I decided to investigate and tried to paraphrase.
When should I praise? What does it do? These thoughts were on my mind.
I heard him say, "Just read my Word, and answers you will find."

So let's begin with why I should; it's based on God above.   (Ps. 118:28)
The Bible states to give God praise for his amazing love.   (Ps. 138:2)
I also praise and thank him that he always answers me.   (Ps. 118:21)
His righteousness, his promises, are why I am set free.   (Pss. 7:17; 56:4)

And praise had more good attributes than I had heard or known,
Lots of reasons I must bring praise before his throne.
It clearly states why praise is good and who should make this choice.
It also lists how I can praise with instruments and voice.   (2Ch 5:13)

Amazing grace, tremendous works, I have my sins washed clean.   (Ps. 9:1; Acts 15:11; Rev. 1:5)
I praise my God for all he's done, of which my eyes have seen.   (Deut. 10:21)
Again, I praise him all day long for all his power and might.   (Pss. 35:28; 21:13)
And I will praise him joyfully; it's pleasing in his sight.   (Ps. 147:1)

The Word shows us that praise and thanks are mighty when combined,   (Neh. 12:46)
So I will praise continually his goal for all humankind.   (Ps. 34:1)
God says that praise is beautiful, with voices loud and clear.   (Ps. 33:1; 2 Chron. 20:19)
Let all men hear my joyful noise, it helps me to draw near.   (Ps. 66:8)

I also praise for how I'm made, his workmanship so grand.   (Ps. 139:14)
He watched as I was in the womb, a marvel of his hand.   (Ps. 139:15)
Let all the earth, and heaven too, sing praises to his name.   (Ps. 69:34)
His praise brings hope, encouragement, a promise I can claim.   (Ps. 42:11)

His mercy is another part of why I must praise him   (2 Chron. 20:21)
For it endures forever more when troubles seem so grim.   (Ps. 56:4)
So praise his name with thanksgiving, and depression it will lift.   (Isa. 61:3)
Sing praises to the Holy One, his joy will pour in swift.

One benefit that praising gives, it helps my soul find rest.

And when I praise he comforts me and helps when I am stressed. (Isa. 12:1)

Praise sets me up with honor, too, and helps defeat my foes (Deut. 26:19)

For God begins to clear my path, and evil plans expose. (2 Chron. 20:22)

Since I believe his Word is true, my hands I start to raise. (Ps. 106:12)

It glorifies my God above as my heart fills with praise. (Pss. 50:23; 9:1)

I'll shout his praise, my Saviour lives, this cannot be ignored. (Ps. 9:14)

I praise his name until I die for Jesus is my Lord. (Ps. 104:33)

Rejoice in the Lord Always

So often we hear why joy is so good, but how do we get it to stay?
Life gives us its trials as problems arise, these things that we face every day.
Now what do we do to overcome this; the Bible can show you and me.
We need to give thanks, rejoice in the Lord for all of his wonders we see. (Ps. 65:8)

For this is the day that our Lord has made, so I will rejoice and be glad. (Ps. 118:24)
From dawn until dusk, from morning to night, rejoice, and his joy he will add. (Neh. 12:43)
As we start to praise and celebrate him, it helps us to not feel so glum. (Deut. 14:26)
Rejoice in the Lord for all he has done and all the great things yet to come. (Joel 2:21)

So let's look at why we rejoice each day and sing with such joy in our heart. (Ps. 71:23)
His mercy is one, his holiness too, good reasons why we should take part. (Ps. 31:7)
And his Word has shown that he'll rescue you; he always gives us one more chance.
Rejoice with your voice, with instruments too, with clapping and even with dance. (Job 21:12)

Exceedingly glad is how we should feel when having our trust in the Lord. (Pss. 68:3; 5:11)
He sees me in pain, my anguish, and tears, and helps me get my life get restored. (Ps. 31:7)
He's faithful and just, our defender too, a guardian who's ready to fight. (Ps. 9:4; Joel 2:23)
For his name is great, the name above names, we tremble with joy at his might. (Pss. 2:11; 21:1)

Rejoice in the Lord for every good thing that he has put into your hands. (Deut. 12:7)
Give praise unto him that he has saved you and paid the price our sin demands. (Rom. 6:23)
Rejoice going in, rejoice going out; he replaces shame with respect. (Isa. 61:7)
And always rejoice that he is our friend, who's closer than we could expect. (Phil. 4:4)

For all those who seek his will every day, rejoice that he dwells in our midst. (1 Chron. 16:10)
Rejoice in the earth—for all that it yields—the fields and the trees that exist. (Ps. 65:8)
For they do rejoice, and heaven above, for he has created all things, (1 Chron. 16:31–32)
And we should rejoice for all we can do, our skills and our talents he brings. (Deut. 12:18)

Rejoice in the Lord for a loving wife, a fountain of blessing for you. (Prov. 5:18)
Give thanks for his Word, a treasure for sure, where daily we find something new. (Ps. 119:162)
Sing unto the Lord, who prepared for us a place that one day we will go. (John 14:2)
For we give him thanks that in his great book, he wrote down our names long ago. (Luke 10:20)

Rejoice for his sake when persecuted, for great is your heavenly gain.   (Matt. 5:12)

For we know the truth—that Satan has lost—the blood of the lamb has domain.   (Rev. 12:11)

So I will rejoice for he is my Lord, and all of his miracles done.   (Ps. 66:6)

For I can't contain this joy deep inside, all glory to Father and Son.

Forgive Yourself

Why would I walk away from things I know the Lord desires?
What causes faith and hope to sag, like nails stuck in my tires?
I think of God, yet make mistakes and always feel regret.
I ask for help in all my prayers, when godly goals aren't met.   (Matt. 26:41)

It seems that there are always things I fail to block and shield.
And when I long for peace and joy, my life's a battlefield.
I want to be close to my Lord, yet sin keeps me apart.   (Gal. 5:17)
I struggle with it in my life yet love him in my heart.

The Word says all have fallen short, that no one measures up.   (Rom 3:23)
But still, I hurt for all my faults, which I need to clean up.
One day I am on fire for God, another I just cope.
Why can't I find a simple way to fill my life with hope?

Sometimes I feel his strength and joy, while others I am weak.
Some days I'm bold and spread his Word, while some I barely speak.
It's like a runner in a race, whose pace can ebb and flow.
I must endure, keep running hard when energy feels low.   (1 Cor. 13:7

For Jesus is our great high priest, he fought temptation's grip.   (Heb. 4:15)
Temptation tried to conquer him but could not make him trip.
He used God's Word to counter what temptation tried to say,
And now he helps us fight this, too, so in God's plan we stay.

We cannot win on our own strength; his Word helps overcome.
So boldly seek forgiveness when to temptation you succumb.   (Heb. 4:16)
For mercy is his strongest trait; the throne of grace awaits.
But guilt and pain will be your friends for he who hesitates.

We need to get back in the game when choices sideline us.
Do not let guilt or shame stop you; God's grace is generous.
Receive his gift, forgive yourself, brush off the dirt, and go.
For God has got a plan for you, where joy and peace will flow.

Our past mistakes never keep us from both his grace and love.   (Rom 8:35)
His peace and grace search out for us, forgiveness from above.
But pain and grief will linger on when past fails stay on shelves.
We are the one who holds us back; we don't forgive ourselves.

Forgiveness is the catalyst that builds relationship.
It brings us peace and happiness as old wounds lose their grip.
We know our deeds come with a price that on this earth we pay.
But Jesus died, and with his blood, the stains are washed away.   (Rev. 1:5)

So you can stand before the Lord and look him in the eye,
Since Jesus stands, our counselor, ready to testify.
So keep the faith and battle on, to be like him our goal.   (Rev 14:12)
Draw on his strength and speak the Word so your life can be whole.

I Am Well Able

It seems to me, in times like this, we feel we lack control.
So many things are happening, it starts to take its toll.
Doubt and worry, fear and stress, attack us every day.
So what do we, as Christians, do to make it go away?

The answer lies within his Word; it tells us what to do.
We know that God is in control, his Word is always true.
Let Jesus guide and be our rock, assurance he will bring.
He sees it all and knows our path, he is the reigning king.

We look at what we face today and think it is so big.
We feel the threat and see the risk, a mighty hole they dig.
But God is huge and knows it all, the future he has mapped.
He says he will protect his own, no matter how we're strapped.

So take control with his command, declare you are well able
To ride the storm and come out strong, his power will enable.
In Exodus, when faced with fear, God told them to endure.
Follow his plan, do what he asked, your faith will then mature.   (Exod. 18:23)

So like the spies who gave report, let yours be full of hope.
Your words should say you're well able; this is your way to cope.   (Num. 13:30)
Don't let doubt in, like all the rest who saw themselves as frail.
For if you think and speak like them, you're surely going to fail.

Trust in the Lord, for he's the one who gives abilities.
But it's our job to use them well, a choice that we must seize.
We serve a God who's well able to do as he desires,
And he made us and gave us gifts to do what he requires.

So face what comes—you can endure—God can and will provide.
Be strong in faith and trust in him, he never leaves our side.
I am able to do all things; my strength comes from the Lord.
I have his Word, his armor too, I wield a mighty sword.

The Fight Within

I knew that God had changed my life the day he died for me.
He paid the price, his sacrifice, so God could set me free.   (1 Cor. 7:23)
I can't repay the gift I got, his blood has made me whole.   (Rom 5:16)
He suffered much for all of us, atonement for our soul.

Now my old self is crucified, and Christ now lives in me.   (Gal. 2:20)
My old desires get traded in for ones inspired by thee.
You loved me so and gave yourself so my relationship
Could be restored with God above; the debt I owe now zip.

It says that when we give our life, that we are born again.
But what is that, what does it mean, what signs should I see then?
The first impact is to my heart, I start to seek his will.
His spirit comes to live within; for me, that is a thrill.

With all he's done, you'd think that I would follow without fail,
When I look at the price he paid, my everlasting bail.
Yet many times I raise the dead, my old self takes a stroll.   (Gal. 5:17)
Emotions reign and tempers flare, I lose my self-control.

It's funny how our old self likes to take offense so fast,
And relish in this selfish state, where hostile feelings last.
I noticed how my thoughts played out, how justified I felt
To blame and rage against my life for what God's hand has dealt.

I know who gives me thoughts like that, the one who seeks my doom.
I also know he can't prevail unless I give him room.
It's up to me to block bad thoughts or let them have their way.
It is my choice, I have free will, to stay or walk away.

So how can I resist this urge to do what self wants done?
The answer comes within his Word, the power from his Son.
Apostle Paul told us the truth, that we can do all things
Through Jesus Christ, who strengthens us, the power his death brings.   (Phil. 4:13)

This is the key to fighting back, wielding the Word itself.

It is the sword that we can hold, don't leave it on a shelf. (Eph. 6:17)

The more you read, the more you know to fight the thoughts you get.

And in that time, when feelings rise, his words you won't forget.

But don't get down when you mess up, it happens to us all.

Just go to him who will forgive, it is the protocol.

Repent and turn and seek his will, get on your knees and pray,

So you can do his will each day, and not get led astray.

He truly is my closest friend, his love's beyond compare.

A closer bond he offers me if I would only dare.

One final thought that makes me smile is God knew I would slip. (Rom. 3:23)

He's faithful to help pick me up and restore fellowship. (1 John 1:9)

Poem Journal: God's Inspiration:
WEEK 25

God's Special Gift

The Word says when a man leaves home, he cleaves unto a wife.   (Gen. 2:24)
But most men seek a friend or mate, not one to change their life.
We fail to see what God has planned, that two become one flesh.
Instead, we try to find someone with common traits that mesh.

Take time to pray, for God knows all, and listen to his voice.
And teach your kids to do the same, so they can find God's choice.
Our God sees in the hearts of all, while we just see their face,
For finding out that we chose wrong leaves scars we can't erase.

I thank the Lord it was his grace that brought my wife to me.
For even though we make a choice, there is no guarantee.
God knows our hearts and what we need to reach our destiny.
I thank the Lord I found a prize with strength and loyalty.

For God says that a good wife is a crown that makes them blessed.   (Prov. 12:4)
A thoughtful wife comes from the Lord; she always does her best.   (Prov. 19:14)
She keeps me on the path I need to go where God has planned.   (Prov. 18:22)
It's good to have a friend so close who likes to hold my hand.

It took me way too long to see what God had seen day 1.
That she was key to my success when all was said and done.
A loving wife, whom God had picked to help me find my way,
Whom I could dance and sing around and hold close when we pray.

So many times I asked the Lord for wisdom in a fight.
Yet somehow, I knew in my heart, our faith would make it right.
For that's the key to finishing strong, together hand in hand,
For in the end if God's put first, together we will stand.

I celebrate this night tonight, now married thirty years,
Since the day we said our vows and many people cheered.
We were so young when we stood there and said, "I do," out loud.
But I could not have asked for more; you always make me proud.

I wrote these words to thank the Lord for giving one so true.
If I could do it all again, I still would choose just you.
I love you, Di, with all my heart, and thank God for his love.
I thank God that he gave me you, a gift from God above. (1 Cor. 7:7)

(An anniversary poem for my wife, Diana.)

Made Alive Again
(Dry Bones)

I often read the prophet's tales and think the stories grand,
How Israel just messed things up and got stuck in the sand.
The movies made these tales of old seem large upon the screen,
But most of us just failed to see what God had wanted seen.

How history repeats itself, of lessons we forgot,
As Hollywood did glamorize, we failed to see God's plot.
It points the way to one who would be crucified for me.
The stories showed how God loved us; he died for all to see.   (John 3:16)

One tale I heard about dry bones was captured in a song,
And I would hum and sing its tune, "dem dry bones," all day long.
I never thought why God did that; I just knew that he could.
But now I know that God did this to show us that he would.

The bones describe our spirit man, when old and spiritually dry,
When we won't do what God has asked, his words we don't apply.
How sin can cause our hearts inside to harden like some stones.
We separate ourselves from God and wither like dry bones.

Ezekiel spoke at God's command to all those bones displayed.   (Ezek. 37:7)
The bones were told to hear God's Word, the first point that he made.   (Ezek. 37:4)
The only way to live again is heeding what he tells,
For no man gets eternal life as long as he rebels.

We must choose first to seek the Lord for Jesus is the way.
The sacrifice that God has made so we have life today.
Ezekiel stood before the bones as God breathed life in them.
They must have been a sight to see, once dead, alive again.

When we accept our Christ as Lord, it says we're made anew.   (John 3:7)
Just like those bones, we are reborn, new people through and through.
This shows how God can save a man, no matter how far gone,
That even in our darkest hour, he brings a brand-new dawn.

It also warns that like the past, God's favor will not stay
If we do not hear what he says and listen and obey.
God's people then abandoned him and struggled with their sin.   (Ezek. 37:11)
And we today are just the same, there is that fight within.

For when our hearts are like dry bones, his breath comes like the wind,   (Ezek. 37:9)
And gives us hope, eternal life, no matter how we sinned.
The Lord has said he surely will cause breath to enter us.
That we should live restored by him, it is so glorious.

The message here is God wants us to know that he is Lord.
When we're with Christ we're made alive, our spirit is restored.
For God has raised us up like bones to stand upon our feet,   (Ezek. 37:10)
And with his breath we can go forth, an army made complete.   (Ezek. 37:14)

The Path of Life

I often think about God's ways; sometimes I lie awake
And think about which way to go, what choices I should make.
God's Word tells us our life is like a winding path ahead,
And how he helps us stay on course if his Word we will imbed.

A path is what we all must choose; the Bible shows us lots.
Pick the right one which honors him, and keep God in all your thoughts.   (Ps. 25:4)
For without God, the path will wind, and traps and snares await.   (Ps. 27:11)
But if God leads, he goes before, the crooked paths made straight.   (Prov. 21:8)

So what do you think you should do, what choice will you pick out?
For many paths await us all, we can't just mill about.   (Prov. 5:21)
Be careful how you choose to go for many paths seem right.   (Prov. 14:12)
But we cannot know which to take; we must have God's insight.

For choosing wrong will lead to death, so we must seek out his will.   (Prov. 14:12)
Let God guide you, and you'll stay safe: Go up and not downhill.   (Prov. 15:24; Isa. 9:6)
There are some signs that we can use to know if we're on course.
The path we choose must put God first for he's the one true source.

Eternal life's a narrow gate, the road is difficult,   (Matt. 7:14)
And many try to find a way but have a bad result.   (Luke 13:24)
But with God's help, he shows the way and makes the road seem wide.   (Prov. 15:19; Ps. 18:36)
For God is good and loves us so, he's always at our side.

The godly path, his Word reveals, is one in which he leads.   (Prov. 3:6)
The evil path is one in which we get stuck in the weeds.   (Prov. 13:6)
But many choose the evil path, and from their God they hide,
And that is why the Bible states the road to doom is wide.   (Matt. 7:13)

The narrow path that God shows us his blessings on its route.
His path is right, it's also safe, it helps us produce fruit.   (Isa. 43:16)
And we can walk a guarded path; we won't get quickly trapped.
His path is smooth, he knows the way, the best path he has mapped.   (Isa. 51:10)

So worry not that you'll be safe if you keep God in sight.
For when we pray and ask his help, we go forth with his might.
Security is what he brings, so we can boldly stride
A path that he has planned for us, a narrow path made wide.

I praise his name for all he does; God guards me with a hedge,   (Job 1:10)
So as I walk along my path, I don't fall off an edge.
He is my God, he loves me so, he watches as I go.
And even when my footing slips, his grace he will bestow.   (Ps. 37:31)

He is the God who lights my path, a lamp unto my feet,   (Ps. 119:105)
And I can go with peace inside, my foes he will defeat.
So praise his name, and honor him for he has blessed me so.
And he will lead or follow me, no matter where I go.

The Power of Prayer

We often hear that we should pray, a tactic we should use.
And when we do it with diligence, good things it will produce.
The Bible speaks of why we should pray often without fail,
For it can cause the Lord to act and help us to prevail.

Jesus told us how we should pray, the Lord's Prayer we recall.
Our Father is the holy God who lives above us all.
His kingdom reigns, his will is done in heaven and on earth.
So I will praise his holy name, and through him I find rebirth.

Each day he gives us food to eat, our daily bread we need,   (Matt. 6:11)
And forgives us when we have sinned, so from this debt we're freed.
Then we forgive, just like he did, the ones who treat us wrong.
Forgiveness helps to free our soul and keep our spirit strong.

He also helps us resist those things that tempt us every day,
And hides us from the evil one by snatching us away.   (Matt. 6:13)
With all these things that God can do, his glory and his might,
We need to pray unceasingly and keep God in our sight.

But prayer is more than just these things, it helps our walk go straight.
We even pray for enemies who persecute and hate.   (Matt. 5:44)
God tells us this is needed so we can be set apart.   (Matt. 5:45)
For only he can change their lives, but we must do our part.

Our secret prayers set forth his plan, his will as he decreed.   (Matt. 6:6)
A harvest lies before us all, but more workers he does need.   (Matt. 9:37)
Prayer is our way to keep us strong, our flesh is often weak,   (Matt. 26:41)
Be willing to let God inside, your heart he will critique.

We do not need a special phone to reach our God above.
Prayer is our link to seek his will and feel his power and love.
With prayer we learn how much he cares and what our life should be.
Filled with his hope and peace and joy, his love has set us free.

So pray and talk to God each day, just like the phone you use.
It's how we talk to our best friend, and he can share his views.
He answers us when we submit, and on our knees we go,
So talk to him about your hurts, and feel his healing flow.

I thank you, Lord, for letting me come close to him this way,
So I can see his precious love each time I start to pray.
For staying close, in prayer each day, revives me when I'm weak.
What other thing compares to this, no other life I seek.

Meditation Explained

As I look into God's Word, his words speak to my heart.
I hear his voice upon my tongue as rhymes inside me start.
Today he spoke about a way to strengthen how I walk,
About a way to stay on course and focus like a hawk.

I know my goal is to bear fruit, a light for all to see,
So what can help me reach this goal, which none can disagree?
One thing I hear him say to me is to read his Word nonstop,
To meditate on what he said, a biblical workshop.

The heroes of the Word of God did meditate all day.
And David stayed awake all night so he could read and pray.   (Ps. 119:148)
Then Joshua did meditate so he would know God's will,   (Josh. 1:8)
And everyone could see God's hand, victories he did fulfill.

Sometimes I hope I say what's right, my teaching is found true,
God said that he'd show me the words if scriptures I did view.   (Luke 21:14)
The Lord said he remembered those who dwelled upon his name,
For those who think about the Lord, he keeps from guilt and shame.

So read and pray and seek the Lord, and keep him top of mind.
Then as you go to work and play, his will you'll surely find.
I meditate upon his Word, his laws, and rules to keep
So I can find a life of joy and have a peaceful sleep.

So many things can fill our mind; our world can make us stressed.
But when we heed his Word each day, he makes our life more blessed.
So we steer clear of life's pitfalls and walk with him beside.
Remember he has chosen us, and for our sins he died.

For this is how we walk with God, his Word upon our lips.
So when we come upon life's trials, his Word can give us tips.
So meditate on godly things, what's just and pure and true.   (Phil. 4:8)
Think on those things of good report, your mind he will renew.

For meditation is the key; it gives us words to say.
When Satan tries to tempt our flesh, God's Word becomes our way.
It helps us dodge the fiery darts the enemy will throw,
And keeps us safe from his attacks, and helps deflect the blow.

So read his Word, a daily goal, so we are strong in him.
It is our light in this dark world when troubles feel so grim.
It helped the saints of old stand firm and does the same today.
Meditate upon his Word, and in God's will you stay.

Poem Journal: God's Inspiration:

WEEK 30

Fruit of the Spirit

I often look for how to live the way God wants me to.
I must obey his Word so that my spirit can renew.
So many times I think I must find ways to set me free,
But God has shown right in his Word his Spirit is the key.

The Spirit has some gifts for us and helps us to bear fruit.   (John 15:5)
So I must read and understand his Word will show the route.
The fruit is what our life brings forth, laid bare for all to see.
Then people know that he's my Lord, and Jesus set me free.

Love and joy are two of them, and they should be our sign.
So people see we follow him, our walk and his align.
When people look at you each day, does your face show you're his?
You should stand out if he's your Lord; it shouldn't take a quiz.

Those two are just the start of what your fruit should show this world.
Your fruit should sprout like an eagle's wings, not closed but stretched unfurled.
We also should show patience and seek a peaceful life,
Not quick to whine or quick to fight for that brings only strife.   (Gal. 6:7)

Patience and peace, the next two fruit, are difficult to find.
For in this world, offense and blame are easily assigned.
Too many folks feel they must fight whenever someone cites
Or says something that they don't like, or tramples on their rights.

There are two roads that we can take, the spirit or the flesh.
Be careful not to focus on a route that does not mesh
With how we must respond when we see things we do not like.
We must seek what the Lord wants us to do before we strike.

Another fruit that helps with this is known as self-control.
It tells us not to jump too quick but search within our soul.
The key is prayer, so we can seek his thoughts on what to do.
When we seek him before all else, his Spirit will shine through.

We know our God is kind and good; these are two fruits as well.
So we must act appropriately so our works also gel
With how our God wants us to be, kindness seen every day,
So our light shines in goodness too so others find his way.   (Gal. 6:10)

Do not be harsh, be gentle too, show mercy like our God.   (Gal. 5:23)
Do not show pride or jealousy, or we look like a fraud.   (Gal. 5:26)
Eternal life is what we want to help the lost obtain.   (Gal. 6:8)
The fruit we have shows all the world our flesh we can restrain.   (Gal. 5:24)

Our gentleness and faithfulness, together hold much weight.
For they show men our walk is just, our flesh we can negate.   (Gal. 5:24)
And just like fruit on trees we see, we want a big windfall,
So when our walk is Spirit-led, these fruits are seen by all.

"If you remain in me and I in you, you will bear much fruit," John 15:5 (NIV)

Cross with grapes growing on it

Who Am I?

The world today goes 'round and 'round at such a frantic pace,
It's hard to know what the truth is about the human race.
The messages are so diverse, with lies that seem so right,
And most are led down foolish paths while looking for the light.

The Word of God tells *who* I am, it states that God made me,
Ephesians shows in great detail for everyone to see.
Man walked away from what God planned and strayed from doing right.
We lost our way as we chose sin, unworthy in his sight.   (Eph. 2:1–3)

He sent his Son to die for me so I could be restored,   (Eph. 1:4)
And showed me who I am in Christ when I call Jesus "Lord."
This was his plan, which he worked out, he chose me in advance.   (Eph. 1:11)
It pleases him to bring me back, and I get a second chance.   (Eph. 1:9)

Now I am blessed to have fellowship with Christ who died for me.   (Eph. 1:3)
I am chosen and adopted into his family.   (Eph. 1:4, 5)
I'm accepted and made holy, his grace poured out on me.   (Eph. 1:6)
I am redeemed; he paid the price, his blood has set me free.   (Eph. 1:7)

I am forgiven by his grace, which he bestows to all,   (Eph. 1:7)
A simple thing for anyone who stops to heed his call.
So I am saved, it is his gift his Spirit in me stored,   (Eph. 2:8)
A newly created masterpiece when I chose him as my Lord.   (Eph. 2:10)

Now I am sealed since I believe the truth his Word reveals.   (Eph. 1:13)
His Spirit is his guarantee, eternal life it seals.   (Eph. 1:14)
I also am a child of God, part of his family,
Which was his plan right from the start for all eternity.   (Eph. 1:11)

So now I know what he has done, it tells me who I am.
It also shows how good God is, and why he sent his lamb.
Now I can boldly state to all, I bow before the King,
And testify to everyone, salvation he did bring.

So never think you are no good, not worthy of his love.
We have a dad who guides our path and watches from above.
So who am I? Why am I here? I answer without doubt,
A child of God saved by his grace is what I proudly shout.

WEEK 32

Be Still, and Know That I Am God

I woke today and ran around at such a hectic pace,
With texts and calls and messages, my brain began to race.
So many things I had to do, it seemed I had no time.
But as I ran and bustled so, my stress began to climb.

Why was my life so hectic now, what made each day so rough?
As COVID-19 hit, the world went nuts, and coping became tough.
I see a lot of people now so stressed and full of fear.
So how do I regain my strength when trouble seems so near?

I left my house with thoughts of work, my mind began to stew,
I felt a wave of worry grow at what I had to do.
And then I heard a small voice say, "Be still for I am God,   (Ps. 46:10)
No matter what the day will bring, my peace is never flawed.   (Isa. 26:3)

"Be still and know that I am God, is how you will survive,
In fact, if I am in your thoughts, good fortune will arrive.
Be still and know that I am God, don't listen to your flesh.
Just focus on my words to you; they'll help your mind refresh.   (Rom. 12:2)

"Be still and know that I am God is how you start your day,
The quietness can center you and help you when you pray.
Be still and know that I am God will let you hear me speak.
My quiet voice will comfort you when you are feeling weak.

"Be still and know that I am God brings peace into your mind.
It helps you deal with problems well and keeps your actions kind.   (1 Pet. 3:8)
Be still and know that I am God is vital for your soul,
It helps you stay on solid ground and keeps you in control.   (Ps. 143:10

"Be still and know that I am God is wisdom in my Word.
It helps you choose the path to take when our sight can be blurred.
For I am in control of all and want you to succeed,   (Prov. 16:3)
But you can only manage this if you will let me lead.

"Be still and know that I am God, for I will show the way.
And I can help you rise above when your mind starts to stray.
So stop, and let your mind be still, get on your knees and wait,
And listen for my still small voice that makes your path stay straight.   (Prov. 4:11)

"Be still and know that I am God is what you have to do.
A principle I give to you, instructions that are true.   (2 Sam. 7:28)
Tell everyone that's in this world, as chaos starts to build,
That much of what is happening is prophecy fulfilled.   (Luke 22:37; 1 Cor. 14:22)

"Be still and know that I am God will keep your mind at peace.
Take in the Word and look to me, anxiety will cease.
Remember that I love you so; I guide and watch your way.   (Ps. 32:8)
And in the end, when you come home, together we will stay."   (2 Cor. 4:14–18)

Take Off Your Mask

I look around the world today, I see a shocking scene.
So many people wearing masks, it is their new routine.
Some think it safe, a good response, a shield while COVID-19 spreads.
They relish this to help feel safe, while others shake their heads.

It makes me think of our response to questions others ask.
Like, "How are you?" "How do you feel?" We start to don our mask.
We hide the things like doubts and fears, and do not let most see
The pain we feel, our burdened hearts, the true reality.

We tell our friends we're doing fine when worry fills our mind.
We wear a mask to hide our pain and struggle on half-blind.
The Bible states that worldly cares can choke God's seed when sown.   (Mark 4:19)
We need to give our cares to God and trust he's on the throne.   (1 Pet. 5:7)

His healing hands will hold you up, his strength he will impart.
So when you pray take off your mask, tell God what's in your heart.
Then trust in him, look deep inside, so he can start his work,
And fill you with his perfect peace, a Holy Spirit perk.   (Gal. 5:22)

The Bible says to talk things out, to share with someone who   (Gal. 6:2)
can give advice from God's own Word and fully support you.   (Eccles. 4:12)
Don't hide your pain, use fellowship, get other saints to pray,   (Eccles. 4:10)
So you can take the mask you wear and cast it far away.

There is a strength that comes when we together stand in prayer.   (Matt. 18:19)
Support and hope are found inside, our burdens we can share.
We fight against a common foe who uses guilt and shame,
To make us wear a spiritual mask, which makes our efforts lame.   (Mark 4:19)

Take off your mask; you are a child of God who rules it all.
Confess your sins, repent to him, then rise and stand up tall.
You have the power deep down inside that comes from God, our King.
Bring out his sword and face the foe, and let God's metal ring.

Rebuke and bind the enemy, there's power in Jesus's name.   (John 20:31)
We serve the Lord who rules it all, his victory I'll proclaim.
My mask is gone; I stand with God, my armor gleaming bright,
And when my foe comes after me, the battle I will fight.   (1 Tim. 6:12)

We have a choice to sit or stand, to fight or to retreat.
God gave us power to fight the foe, not hide and take a seat.
Look inside and see the might, the power that God can bring.
We fight a foe already beat, which makes my spirit sing.

Yet Satan tries to douse our hope with lies and his deceit.
For he knows well the day will come when all see his defeat.
I'll spread the Word to all who'll hear, its hope and peace I bring.
For in the end, all knees shall bow and call our Lord the King.   (Isa. 45:23; Rom. 14:11)

Stay Focused

With everything we face today, with all the points of view,
Priorities get set aside; we do not follow through.
The news, our phones, our emails, too, can overwhelm the best
And cause us to stay up at night, and not get needed rest.

Don't let the world use up your time on things that fade away.　　　(1 Tim. 4:7)
It is our goal, our purpose here, to reach the lost today.　　　(Mark 16:15)
Why do we let these minor things take up our precious time?
They can become our focal point and cause our stress to climb.

We know he says what we should do; he waits for us to choose　　　(Isa. 30:18)
To follow him and seek his will and listen to his cues.
We need to look inside ourselves, at why we get bogged down,
And what we must give focus to from morn until sundown.

The trouble is most do not know that peace is what God brings,
And we cannot give hope to them when wasting time on things.
They do not help us follow what the Lord wants us to do,
So set your sights on what God says, the things that he calls true.　　　(1 Cor. 7:35)

The Word of God gives warning that the enemy will try　　　(Mark 13:5)
To distract us and make us choose the things that satisfy.
Our fleshly needs, addictions too, can keep us from his call
To be a light unto the world and bring good news to all.

And through it all, we can forget what God wants us to do.
He has a goal that we should seek a plan we should pursue.
For God has said, "I set you free, stand tall for you're my child."　　　(Rom. 6:22)
Instead, we sink our heads in shame, as though we've been exiled.

The enemy roams 'round the earth with lies to keep men snared.　　　(1 Pet. 5:8)
He makes us sit instead of fight, both guilt and shame impaired
With lies that we are too far gone, that we have failed too much,
That we don't deserve the grace of God, so we stay in his clutch.

Don't listen to his lies again, but let your hope renew.
Pick up the sword, get in the game, his lies you can subdue.
Know your role and who you are; remember why we're here—
To save a world that's lost today in suffering and fear.

Shake off your fear, your guilt, and shame; repent and lose the doubt.
Then open wide your heart to him so he can clean it out.
Just pray and seek the Lord each day, and your mind he will renew.
Then tell the world he is the light, the rock they can cling to.   (Luke 6:48)

No greater goal has he set forth for all who do believe,
To tell humankind they can be saved if Jesus they receive.
He is the hope, the peace, and the joy that our world needs to find.
Our mandate is to spread the Word, so none get left behind.

Poem Journal: God's Inspiration:

WEEK 35

A Judas Kiss

"Judas" is the term we use for those who betray friends,
A person who brings lots of pain and never makes amends.
A person who acts like a friend but betrays with a kiss,   (Matt. 26:48–50)
Who leaves a hurt down deep inside when things have gone amiss.

But often they are part of life for which God has a plan.
We only see the hurt and pain, not what our God began.
Remember that he sees it all; he knows where we should go.   (Job 34:21; Prov. 5:21)
What Satan means to cause us harm, God uses for his show.   (Gen. 50:21)

Adversity must come to all who seek his will each day.   (Job 2:10)
The enemy will try to stop God's blessings sent our way.
Rejoice and praise our God above for he makes our way straight.   (Luke 3:5)
His mercy always follows us; it is his greatest trait.   (Ps. 23:6)

God lets a Judas in our life and lets us suffer loss   (2 Tim. 3:12)
So God can then complete his plan, like Jesus at the cross.   (Col. 2:2)
In all your ways acknowledge him, he will direct your path.   (Isa. 26:7; Prov. 3:6)
He's in control for good and bad, don't try to do the math.

Betrayal can adjust our path and take us where God wants.
But Satan tries to take us down, with doubt and fear he taunts.   (Ps. 27:11)
When Judas kissed the cheek of Christ, he thought he brought him down, (Ps. 5:8)
But God would use betrayal's sting to lead him to his crown.

So trust that God has got a plan with blessings set for you.   (Eccles. 11:5)
When life looks bleak and hope is weak, hold fast to his promise true.
And let his Word encourage you and brighten up your day.   (Ps. 119:35)
Just thank the Lord and praise his name, then peace will come your way.

God rules it all, a sovereign Lord, which lets me boldly say,   (2 Sam. 7:22)
No matter what gets thrown my way, God has the final say.
A Judas is a stepping stone that God puts at our feet.
So trust in him, he has a plan, our God cannot be beat.   (Ps. 145:3)

And Two Shall become One

A marriage is a covenant
where both must seek God's will.
Just put him first and read his Word,
your hearts he will infill.

His gifts will help you walk as one;
your minds they will protect.
So you can stay as one in him,
your paths he will direct.

The Spirit's gifts will teach you how
to love as God would do.
Then when you feel that times are tough,
his Word will speak to you.

Just keep him as your focal point,
and closer you will get.
Make him the center of your life,
your needs will all be met.

(For Raymond and Caroline, who renewed their vows August 2, 2020.)

Dare to Believe

The Bible says that by his stripes, his healing we receive.   (Isa. 53:5)
Do you still need a healing touch? You must dare to believe.
Does worry and anxiety feel like there's no reprieve?
Our God is called the Prince of Peace, simply dare to believe.   (Isa. 9:6)

Hope comes first, then faith comes next; trust that his Word is true,   (1 Thess. 5:8)
Dare to believe that our God wants the best for me and you.
To trust in God is more than words, it's actions that we do.
Step out in faith and seek his face, and he will uplift you.

He is the same throughout all time, your fears he will relieve.
He always keeps his promises if you dare to believe.
Just focus on what he tells you, not what your mind tells you.
He is the God who rules it all, his promises are true.   (2 Sam. 22:31)

Faith is knowing that our God will do what he has said.
So listen to the Spirit's voice, and go where he has led.
To firmly trust will be my goal so I can please the Lord   (Prov. 3:5)
And boldly go before his throne, where peace is my reward.

I know that often when we pray we do not see a change,
But faith is knowing it will come, all things he can arrange.   (Heb. 11:1)
So how do you keep faith alive, to stay strong while you wait?
The key is knowing God's got this, his time is never late.   (Exod. 9:5; Ps. 102:3)

Let go of how you think it should appear or come to pass.
God is working behind the scenes; his planning is first class.   (Ps. 74:12; Eccles. 8:17)
Think of the times he's fought for you, his promises do cleave,
And he will strengthen your resolve if you dare to believe.

Poem Journal: God's Inspiration:
WEEK 38

Life 2.0

The modern world is changing fast as new things are designed.
Technology keeps ramping up so quickly we fall behind.
Most people own computers now, a modern tool they trust.
While some don't use them much at all, for most they are a must.

Its software tells us what to do when any key is pressed.
A programmer has designed it to run at its best.
But over time, it can slow down and sometimes fail to work.
Corrupted data can occur if viruses do lurk.

Computer techs can clean them out; they know the files to seek.
They also update software so it runs at its peak.
I compare this to our own lives and how we run our race.
Our minds get cluttered with bad stuff when we don't seek God's face.   (2 Tim. 1:7)

We start to focus on the wrong things that make us go off course.
We fail to heed what God tells us, which leads to much remorse.
The Holy Spirit is our tech; he lets us know what's wrong.
So heed the voice you hear inside, and troubles won't last long.

The Bible is the tech manual when viruses invade.
Our God designed the hardware, too, for by his hands we're made.   (Ps. 139:14)
So only he can fix the bugs that we let in our mind,
Then we can live the life he planned, our system he designed.

Let him renew what's in your mind each day a fresh new start,   (Rom. 12:2)
A better version of yourself, with an upgraded heart.   (Phil. 2:5)
His Word says dwell on good reports, don't focus on the bad.   (Phil. 4:8)
So you can stay in tune with God and in your soul be glad.

A better life is what he gives when your mind he restarts,   (1 Cor. 2:16)
Just read his Word and meditate, he'll clean infected parts.
Then you can live as he designed once you've sanitized,
He is the tech who knows it all; your mind's been optimized.

Rise Up

I close my eyes to meditate and listen for his voice.
Inside myself I hear a thought, *It's time to make a choice!*
It seems to me that I am drawn to scenes within my head,
Where battle lines are forming fast while I lay in my bed.

I hear a voice that penetrates the scene I watch unfold.
Rise up, my child, and grab your sword, it's time to stand up bold!   (Eph. 5:14)
I see a crown with mangled barbs, I touch a bloody thorn.
It is from Christ, who sacrificed so I could be reborn.   (John 1:13)

I see the sword, which is his Word, it glows like molten steel.   (Eph. 6:17)
The power of his blood runs through, a vibrancy I feel.
I see an angel standing there, a warrior so fierce,   (Exod. 15:3)
I have the urge to close my eyes, my soul his gaze does pierce.

Again, I hear the phrase repeat, "Rise up, rise up my child,
It's time to get your armor on"; I glance to where it's piled.   (Eph. 6:13)
He tells me we are in a war, yet most don't realize.
Though he's been calling out their name, they're fooled by Satan's lies.   (Matt. 24:5; Rev. 3:3)

He blows a horn and shouts aloud, "Rise up, oh mighty men!"   (1 Cor. 14:8)
I start to watch his children rise, first one, then five, then ten.
The breath of God can raise dry bones, a sight I'd love to see.   (Ezek. 37:4)
I watch the children of the Lord become a great army.   (Zech. 10:5

He tells me that I need to rise and use his name with might.
But most of all, I need to pray so more will rise and fight.
The battle is upon us now; be bold and do not cower.
For Satan is a roaring lion, seeking to devour.   (1 Pet. 5:8)

We look around the world today; it's not a pretty sight.
It's easy to just sit and stare and not rise up and fight.
Distraction is his way to stop the children of the Lord.
We focus on the world around and don't pick up our sword.   (Titus 3:3)

The battle is around us now, we must join in the fray.
The best defense is in the Word: Get on your knees and pray.
It is not flesh, nor is it blood that comes against with might,   (Eph. 6:12)
The enemy attacks us all, and we must prepare to fight.

But who can stand against our God, as radiant as the sun.
The outcome has been written down; he has already won.   (Rev. 12:8)
A final thought goes through my mind: It was for me he died.
This mighty God can do all things yet wants me at his side.   (Rev. 17:14)

Humility

We serve a God who strengthens us, he helps us every day.
But we must all still do our part when struggles come our way.
No matter how we need God's help, we need to look inside,
A stumbling block that many have is foolish human pride.   (Prov. 11:2)

The Bible states that pride is like a chain around our neck,   (Ps. 73:6)
Which lets in darkness and chaos that make our life a wreck.
But God will rescue those who kneel and let God take control.   (Ps. 18:27)
For only when he is our Lord, can our hearts be made whole.

Humility is what we need, the secret to success.
We need to let God lead our life and all our sins confess.
For only then can we achieve the breakthroughs that we need,   (Ps. 149:4)
The Bible shows us this is true in both our word and deed.   (James 3:13; Titus 3:2)

Like Naaman, who had leprosy and sought a healing touch,   (2 Kings 5:1–14)
He talked with healers all the time; they could not help him much.
Though he commanded many men, had favor with the king,
He heeded what his servant said, a task quite humbling.

She told him of a prophet who could help him be restored.
So he set out to talk to him, but status was ignored.
Elisha had no time for him—he was a busy man—
An assistant came to tell Naaman about Elisha's plan.

But Naaman was not happy with the treatment that he got.
He wanted to turn back that day, his anger grew white hot.
Again, his servants counseled him to heed these words and stay.
He almost missed his miracle when pride got in the way.

Once again he listened to the sage advice at hand.
He finally did what he was asked, just as the task was planned.
He bathed himself, all seven times, while servants did look on.
And when he rose the seventh time, the leprosy was gone.

He had to learn humility, so vital at this part,   (Luke 14:11)
For trusting what the prophet said would let the healing start.
The point was not the task at hand but if he would obey,
And not give in to prideful thoughts and simply walk away.

So when you ask the Lord for things, be careful how you ask.
Be sure you're cloaked with humbleness, take off the prideful mask.   (Col. 3:12)
Then give God room to do his thing, especially when you pray.
He still completes his promises though we can't see a way.

God takes the lowly and the meek and lifts their heads high,   (Matt. 23:12)
And smites the mighty, full of pride, who mock him and defy.
Grace and honor follow those who kneel before the King,   (1 Pet. 5:5)
But arrogance and prideful ways, destruction they will bring.   (Prov. 16:18)

The Bible tells a parable about a wayward son   (Luke 15:11–24)
Who takes the portion saved for him to party and have fun.
He spends it all, none is left, and ends up in despair.
He thought he had no chance at all, a life beyond repair.

But suddenly it came to him, *Think back on your childhood,*
Where in your house there was no lack, your servants had it good.
He then heads home without much hope, expecting he'll be shunned,
But sees his dad, who runs to him, this greeting leaves him stunned.

His father represents our God, who knows we go astray,   (Isa. 53:6)
Who welcomes us with open arms, forgiveness is his way.   (Matt. 18:13)
Humility is how we show that God is also Lord,
For only when we bow our knee can honor be restored.   (Prov. 15:33; 18:12)

God's power flows when we submit with blessings he has stored.   (Prov. 22:4)
It lets God heal our broken lives when we're in accord.
Humble yourself, and you will find your spirit truly thrives.   (Prov. 29:3)
Humility's the catalyst to turn around our lives.

Bolder Faith

When we lack faith or trust in God, it brings both pain and strife.
Faith, by itself, is not enough; good deeds bring it to life.   (James 2:17, 22)
We're saved by faith, made whole by faith, the currency of God.   (Luke 17:19)
Apostles asked for greater faith, an act I can applaud.   (Luke 17:5; 18:42)

I want that bolder kind of faith that listens when he calls.   (Ps. 85:8; Prov. 4:10)
I need that bolder kind of faith that leaps before it crawls.
I want that bolder kind of faith that seeks his face each day.   (Heb. 11:6)
I need that bolder kind of faith that comes out when I pray.   (James 5:15)

The Bible shows us many men who spoke their faith aloud,
The type of faith that Jesus used to feed the hungry crowd.   (Mark 6:38–44)
Our faith is used to do God's will, the groundwork we require.
It helped three teens to trust in God when thrown into the fire.   (Dan. 3:23)

I want that bolder kind of faith that knows his Word is true,
I need that bolder kind of faith his Spirit can flow through.
I want that bolder kind of faith where in my God I boast.   (Pss. 20:7; 34:2)
I need that bolder kind of faith that makes no sense to most.

We're justified by faith alone, and the righteousness it brings.   (Rom 3:30; 4:5–9)
Faith purifies our heart each day, with it my spirit sings.   (Acts 15:9; Ps. 51:14)
So ask the Lord for greater faith so you can walk in peace.
You're his creation, made for this, you are a masterpiece.   (Eph. 2:10)

I want that bolder kind of faith that speaks his promises.
I need that bolder kind of faith that through me witnesses.
I want that bolder kind of faith that operates with love.   (1 Cor. 13:13)
I need that bolder kind of faith that comes from God above.

Our faith is how we're saved by grace, a gift for all to see.   (Eph. 2:8)
A greater faith should be our goal, so our trust is in thee.
A type of faith that God bestows on those he calls his heirs,   (Titus 3:7)
A type of faith that rises up and puts down worldly cares.

I want that bolder kind of faith that keeps me up at night.   (Acts 18:9; 27:23)
I need that bolder kind of faith that makes me stand and fight.   (2 Tim. 4:7)
I seek that bolder kind of faith that never gets worn out.   (Heb. 12:3)
I need that bolder kind of faith that people call far-out.

The kind of faith that comes from God, and comes from him alone,   (1 Cor. 12:9)
That makes us stronger, full of peace, a type that we can hone.
I want that bold, unmoving faith that keeps my hope intact,   (Col. 1:23)
The kind of faith that hears God's voice but also makes me act.

I want that bolder kind of faith, so strong it never cracks.
I need that bolder kind of faith I read about in Acts.
I want that bolder kind of faith so I can do his will.
I need that bolder kind of faith that his Word can instill.

Strong faith from God is what I need, the kind that won't back down.
The healing faith a woman showed when she just touched his gown.   (Mark 5:25–34)
Our faith is like a mustard seed that starts off very small,
But branches out to shelter us, a great tree that is tall.   (Luke 13:19)

I want that bolder kind of faith that makes the mountain move.
I need that bolder kind of faith with which his Word I prove.
I want to get that kind of faith that stirs his gifts in me.   (Ps. 45:1)
I need that bolder kind of faith that trusts before I see.   (Heb. 11:1)

I thank God for all he has done, for his inspiration and gift of poetry he   (Ps. 45:1)
has put in me.

Promises

I must declare God's promises if I expect to see
They manifest within my life, for speaking them is key.   (Pss. 19:14; 107:2)
Thinking good thoughts is helpful, too, a path we need to seek
Since God will often go to work when we begin to speak.   (Ps. 54:2)

It is how God created things; he spoke, and it became.   (Gen. 1:9)
And his Word states that we have power when we speak out his name.
Our words can bless, or they can curse, in heaven or on earth.
So choose your words most carefully; don't minimize their worth.   (Ps. 141:3)

When you speak out, do you make great your problems or your God,   (Acts 4:20)
Since magnifying problems makes your prayer requests quite flawed?   (James 1:6, 7)
So speak out words, his promises, what you want to unfold,
And do not beg or whine to God; declare his blessings bold.

Like Abraham, who looked not at his age or circumstance,   (Rom. 4:19)
Who did not waiver, even when there didn't seem a chance.
He held the promise given him, regardless of his state,
And Sarah bore the promised son; God never does things late.   (Gen. 21:7)

He promises to be with you and never leave your side.   (John 14:16)
He promises eternal life; it was for you he died.
He promises if you seek him, you will find him indeed.   (Prov. 8:17)
He promises to rescue you if his Word you will heed.

He promises to give you strength when we ourselves have none.   (Isa. 40:29; Phil. 4:13)
So many blessings you can have when you accept his Son.
King David spoke about his God, he praised his holy name,
For only God can save your soul and take away the blame.

So speak and shout about your God, for all he's done for you.   (Isa. 63:7)
Words have power, so use them well; his promises are true.
Remember that your words bring life, speak out his Word aloud.
Speak to your problems with his Word, and watch yourself be wowed.

You are a child of our great God, declare his blessings true.
And even when you see no way, God makes a way for you.
Praise God for all that he will do, come boldly to his throne.
Hold fast your faith; God will not fail, his promises you own.

(1 Cor. 10:13)
(Eph. 3:12; Heb. 4:16)

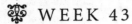
When I Feel Weak

Sometimes it's hard to find the strength to do what must be done.
God knew our lives would have its trials; it's why he sent his Son.
You're not alone, I feel it too; each person gets this way.
A battle forms within our minds, our hopes begin to fray.

The simple truth is we think small; we need our view enlarged.
So where do I renew my strength? How can I get recharged?
The Bible gives us useful tools since God has planned a way
To build our strength and regain hope; just ask for strength each day.

The Bible says he's always there when we need him the most.
Plus, Jesus knew that we'd need help, so he sent the Holy Ghost.
The Holy Spirit lives within to help us battle through,
So when you're feeling weak inside, His power can renew.

If you feel weak, say you are strong; it's what the scriptures say.   (Joel 3:10)
And trust the Lord will keep his word when you begin to pray.   (Ps. 42:11)
The garment of our praise to him surrounds us when we're sad.   (Isa. 61:3)
Just sing and shout and praise his name, and soon you will feel glad.

He will renew your strength as well, like eagles you will soar.   (Isa. 40:31)
Cast all your cares upon the Lord, your peace he will restore.
The key is waiting on the Lord; let him direct your ways.   (2 Chron. 15:7)
Put down the flesh and do his will and keep him in your praise.   (Isa. 35:4)

The Bible tells us many times to stay strong and not dismayed.   (2 Chron. 32:7; Prov. 18:10)
Use wisdom found in God's own Word, and strength shall be displayed.   (Prov. 24:5)
The joy God brings will strengthen you, your weeping won't last long.   (Neh. 8:10; Ps. 30:5)
Think on those things the Lord has done; dwell not on what is wrong.   (Phil. 4:8)

The oil of joy replaces grief, so sadness won't stop you   (Isa. 61:3)
From moving on when life gets hard, and you can start anew.
The joy comes from the price he paid, the key to our success.
With him we have eternal life, salvation we possess.

In all of this we need to know no problem is too large.
We simply go to God in prayer, our strength he will recharge.
Just keep your gaze on his face, and fill your lips with praise.
No matter what will come your way, your hope and strength he'll raise.

A Fish Story
(Book of Jonah)

When people think of Jonah's tale, they think about a whale.
They seldom think about just why this prophet chose to fail.
We rarely look at what transpired to make him run away.
If God asked us to go there too, what answer would we say?

If God asked you to preach in slums, would you say yes or no?
For Nineveh was not a place that most would want to go.
It represents the toughest streets, where good folks never went.
It reeked of death, a place reviled, would you go if you're sent?

Would you be willing to share God with people like those here?
Would you go to the worst of men, or would you disappear?
It's easy to judge Jonah when we sit upon a pew,
But in the grime and violent towns, could God rely on you?

It makes me search inside myself and makes me feel such guilt.
For many times I could have stopped but watched my courage wilt.
I need my Lord to change my heart so it craves saving souls.
To have the strength to go where sent must be one of my goals.

Lord, give me strength and firm resolve to listen to your voice,
And unlike Jonah, go where led, which is the proper choice.
The story here is not the whale; why make the tale so grand?
The key is not that it ate him but how he saw dry land.

The mercy of the Lord is key; he knows we will steer wrong.
It shows the lengths the Lord will take to keep us safe and strong.
To listen close and go where asked is hard for us to do.
To stretch our faith and trust in him is tough for me and you.

Our biggest goal should be to tell the world about our Lord,
So they can find eternal life, relationship restored.
Lord, help me go where you direct to save those who are lost.
This is our calling, as his saints, no matter what the cost.

Although it sounds like a straightforward plan, it's hard to make it stick.
For trusting in the Lord each day is not an easy trick.
The biggest thing is look inside, your weakness he will show.
And pray for courage in your walk and trust when he says go!

Family

My family is the greatest gift that God has given me.
A father, husband, shepherd, too, is what I need to be.
God is the dad I want to be, his traits I want to show.
For in this world that's gone astray, he points which way to go.

My children are gifts from God, gifts beyond compare.   (Ps. 127:3)
No matter what mistakes they make, the pain I gladly bear.
Just as our God shows mercy still when we have gone astray,   (Ps. 86:15)
My love for them will never dim, it strengthens every day.

My wife is one of God's great gifts to which I hold on tight.   (1 Cor. 7:7)
For she completes my heart and soul and makes each day so bright.
I sometimes fail to cherish that, her worth I fail to see.
Then God points out how he made her the perfect one for me.   (Prov. 5:18)

I look at God, his attributes, and think about how we should be
A family in accord with love and unity.   (Phil. 2:2)
Our house stands strong when we all pray, our roots in God run deep.
When problems come, we climb them all, no matter if they're steep.

Plus, this is how our church should be, a family standing strong,
Not fight and argue all the time; to me, that is simply wrong.
As Christ loved us, we should respond and focus on his Word.   (Phil. 1:27)
So when our foe comes after us, together we are stirred.   (Isa. 50:8)

We have a dad who sacrificed his Son for you and me,
Who watched him mocked, betrayed, and killed when hung upon a tree. (Matt. 27:29–30)
It makes me think about my kids and gives me such a chill.
How could a dad watch what took place up on Golgotha's Hill?   (John 19:17)

I simply cannot understand how God felt at this loss.
The Trinity was split apart, divided at the cross.   (Matt. 27:46)
It's why my heart now cherishes all those in my life,
For losing those you hold most dear cuts deeper than a knife.

Yet some today just look away while unborn lives are lost.
Our world seems not to realize the price this act will cost.
The broken souls, the pain and grief a mother must go through,
How God must weep when he sees this, they know not what they do.

But many do not share this love with families in their life.
They've battled through abuse and hate with broken hearts and strife.
To those, he gives renewed beauty if they will trust in him.   (Isa. 61:3)
He takes their pain and vindicates, revives their light grown dim.   (Ps. 26:1)

So never take for granted those God puts in front of you.
It's not by chance, it was his plan, you merely never knew.
He gives the broken a fresh start; he sets the captives free.
When you're with Christ, you're brought into the perfect family.

When you are his, a child of God, you have a dad above,
The perfect dad who never fails, who shows his perfect love.   (Ps. 18:30)
You have a friend, the Bible says, who's closer than your bro.   (Prov. 18:24)
He never leaves and loves you more than you could ever know.

So when you think about family, just look to God above.
He sent his Son—no greater gift—the marvel of his love.
And when you're down and feel alone, God's family is there,
The Father, Son, and Spirit, too, their love beyond compare.

The Power to Stand

So when we pray to God above, how do we not show doubt?
For many people pray for things but fail to wait it out.
To stand when all our senses say it simply won't come true,
It's harder than you think it is, and a battle will ensue.

We battle not just flesh and blood but evil powers too.   (Eph. 6:12)
So God tells us that when we stand, let courage pull us through.   (1 Cor. 16:13)
The key is knowing that our God is faithful in all things,   (Deut. 7:9)
He is the same, he does not change, his promises he brings.

And how do we stay strong in faith when we can't see results?
For doubt and shame are what we learned when we became adults.
His Word is how we know his will and how to stand up strong.   (1 Cor. 15:1)
Trust in the Lord, not what you think, and things will not go wrong.   (Prov. 3:5)

The traits of God we need to know and trust in every day.
His mercy and his grace surround and cause our hope to stay.   (Rom. 5:2)
But there is more that we can do to help us while we wait,
His Word gives us some spiritual tools, his belt and his breastplate.   (Eph. 6:14)

For truth we gird about ourselves to keep our hope intact.
And righteousness will focus us, so our faith can't be cracked.
For when we trust in God alone, he gives us strength to stand.   (Rom. 14:4)
Then stand and watch what he can do, all things he does command.   (Luke 8:25)

Be careful not to listen to advice that people say.
If it is not what God told you, it can cause you to stray.   (1 Cor. 2:5)
His armor will help us stay strong when Satan tells us lies.   (Eph. 6:11)
So we can stand, then stand some more, no matter how he tries.   (Eph. 6:13)

The liberty that God gives us can break the yoke of guilt   (Gal. 5:1)
And keep us from believing lies that cause our faith to wilt.
Our faith is how we trust in him when we don't see a way,   (Heb. 11:1)
And hold fast to your joy in him and praise him every day.   (2 Cor. 1:24)

His Word tells us to stand as one, in spirit we unite.
We reinforce a person's faith so they can stand and fight.
For there is power when we join hands, his presence will descend.
And in his glory and his strength, we'll stand until the end.

One thing that we have learned from this: God always has a plan.
Don't listen to the devil's lies; he caused the fall of man.
You also do not have to try to do it all alone.
Get on your knees and bow your head, come boldly to his throne.

We all will face adversity, and at times it seems unfair.
Some trials and tests come at us quickly; we find it hard to bear.
But he provides his strength to us to help us make it through.
And when we finally see success, there's good news there for you.

Like Moses when he left Egypt, the struggle seemed too much.
Yet he told all the Israelites these words that you can clutch.
The enemies you see today you'll never see again.   (Exod. 14:13)
So with God's help, we'll overcome; we just don't know the when!

So do not let your senses rule; trust him who made us all.   (Isa. 29:16)
When standing feels like it's too tough, his strength won't let you fall.
No matter what you face in life, our God is always there.   (Heb. 13:5)
He's greater than the world around, no other can compare.   (Phil. 2:9)

Giving Thanks

The world we're in loves holidays, a time to reminisce,
Where families go and spend some time to be with ones they miss.
Thanksgiving is a special time when gravy always flows.
When turkey fills us to the brim and then makes us start to doze.

When I grew up, my dad said grace and spoke of what we had
And why we should be thankful, too, since others had it bad.
And after that we ate and drank and carried on 'til late.
Then off to bed to say our prayers and sleep off all we ate.

But rarely did we open wide the book that told us why,
And really look at what God did and all he did supply.
For Thanksgiving is more than food; it's honoring our Lord.   (Ps. 92:1)
We're thanking him for all he does, and this should not be ignored.

The Bible says we must do this, his will for all the saints.   (1 Thess. 5:8)
We need to come before our King with thanks and not complaints.
A thankful heart is what we need to start each day out right.
It's how we start to meditate; it's pleasing in his sight.   (Ps. 100:4)

The Bible says to thank the Lord by telling everyone   (1 Chron. 16:8)
Of all the things that we have seen and all that he has done.
We thank the Lord that he is good and for his holiness,   (Ps. 30:4)
That grace and mercy follow us for all of our success.   (1 Chron. 16:34)

We thank the Lord that he is wise, his judgments always sound.   (Ps. 119:62)
That he is always near to us when trouble does abound.   (Ps. 75:1)
Give thanks to him who made it all—the heavens and the earth—   (Ps. 136:5, 6)
Who spoke and flung the stars above, our galaxy's own birth.   (Ps. 136:7)

Give thanks for how he keeps us safe and all our answered prayers.   (2 Cor. 1:11)
Give thanks for his eternal love; it shows how much he cares.   (1 Chron. 16:34)
So many times he guides our steps in ways we cannot tell.
Not only does he care for us, he helps our kids as well.   (Ps. 107:21)

We need to thank him with our words, but also in our deeds.   (Col. 3:17)
So live a life that honors him, and follow where he leads.
Then thank the Lord for everyone that God has sent your way.   (Rom. 1:21)
He puts them there to bless your life, so thank him when you pray.   (Phil. 1:3)

A key to staying close to God is thankfulness and praise.
If thanks and praise aren't in our heart, our life can go sideways
For knowing God is not enough, he must be glorified.   (Rom 1:21)
For if we stop our hearts grow dark and cause us to backslide.

So thanking God is more than just politeness and respect.
It is a weapon we can use to fix a disconnect.   (Isa. 51:3)
The peace we feel when close to him can help our wounds to heal,
And give us strength to face each day with energy and zeal.

I thank that I have heard his voice, his salvation now I know.   (1 Thess. 2:13)
I thank the Lord he is my strength, a shield against my foe.   (Ps. 28:7)
I thank him that he brings me peace that stays within my heart.   (Col. 3:15)
I thank him that he guards my mind, his Word he will impart.   (Phil 4:7)

I thank him that he rules it all; he reigns and has great might.   (Rev. 11:17)
His wonders I will talk about, his miracles recite.   (Pss. 136:4; 26:7)
The Bible says to never stop, to thank him all the time.   (Ps. 75:9)
So I will sing and praise his name, and thank him with this rhyme.

A Heart Like God

The world comes at me fast each day and often is unkind.
I get defensive and upset, and anger fills my mind.
So this is why the Bible says to guard our hearts and minds   (Phil. 4:7)
For bitterness is like a root, around our heart it twines.   (Heb. 12:15)

One trait of God is tenderness, compassion when we fall.   (James 5:11, NLT)
It's why he sent his Son to die, compassion shown for all.   (Phil. 2:1)
Yet how do I react to those whose lives can be a mess?
Sometimes my heart grows cold to them, a sin I must confess.   (Prov. 24:17)

A tender heart that's filled with love is God's will for my life.
For when I have a hardened heart, it brings much pain and strife.   (Rom. 1:21)
My actions must portray God's love, especially when I hurt,
For angry words not filled with love will never help convert.   (James 1:26)

So how do I protect my heart so mercy guides my way?   (Prov. 4:23)
I start by asking God to help, to cleanse it when I pray.   (Ps. 27:14)
Forgiving those who treat me bad, a struggle I go through,   (Matt. 6:14)
Like Christ had said, I need to see they know not what they do.   (Luke 23:34)

How many weep for those around who do not know the Lord?   (Jer. 7:29; 2 Kings 22:19)
How many yearn to save the World with love wrapped 'round their sword?
The Word of God, which is our sword, can show he is the way.
But if we club them with his book, they simply turn away.

Only God can resurrect a spirit that is dead.
Then once reborn and made anew, their graveclothes they must shed.
Like Lazarus, who came alive, but still was wrapped up tight,   (John 11:44)
A person saved can still be bound, there is a spiritual fight.

To help unwrap what's kept them bound, the saints must do their part.
For this is where they're most at risk, and we need a tender heart.   (Matt. 13:5, 6)
Encourage them to read God's Word—it helps them fix what's wrong—   (Josh. 1:8)
But understand they're in a fight, and some bondages are strong.

This does not mean we accept sin; it needs to be addressed.
We must show love when we correct, so they don't get distressed.
If all we do is raise our voice, we're doing something wrong.
The Bible says that without love, we're like a clanging gong.   (1 Cor. 13:1)

Frustration is a normal thing when we can't see success.
Just realize that with some folks, we must use tenderness.
For only God sees in their heart; he sees what we cannot.   (Luke 16:15)
The biggest thing that we can do is pray for them a lot.

Lord, let my heart stay soft inside; please help me stay that way
So I will yearn to save the lost, your focus every day.   (Luke 15:4)
Help me to coach but not to judge, like your Word warns us all,   (Matt. 7:1; Luke 6:37)
So I can help to lift those up who stumble, slip, and fall.

The Cross

I have a picture in my mind of what the cross was like,
And when I hear about the cross, emotions start to spike.
It is the symbol people wear to show what they've believed,
Yet many failed to understand all that the cross achieved.

One thing we see that Jesus did was carry his own cross.   (John 19:17)
How many people carry now their sin, their pain, and loss?
It tells me that I should discard those things that weigh me down.
The Bible says to cling to God so nothing steals my crown.   (Rev. 3:11)

Next, as I search the Holy Book, I see a central theme:
God had a plan right from the start for souls he would redeem.   (Eph. 3:6)
He sent his Son to die for us upon a wooden cross   (John 3:16)
To pay the price for all humankind, a debt of sin and loss.   (Isa. 44:22)

His sacrifice was so extreme, I cannot comprehend
What he endured to pay my debt; I'll find no better friend.
For at the cross where he was slain, his purpose was fulfilled.   (Matt. 8:17; 2 Cor. 1:20)
My sin is gone, got washed away when Jesus's blood was spilled.   (Rev. 1:5; 1 Cor. 6:11)

The agony that he endured is more than I could bear.
Imagine what the scene looked like if you were standing there.
It makes my heart want to explode; it is too much for me.
The gruesome scene that did unfold, I wouldn't want to see.

For he was nailed upon a tree, the spikes right through his hands.   (Acts 2:23)
A crown of thorns stuck on his head, all part of God's own plans.   (Matt. 27:29)
The cross became the focal point; his death had paid the price.   (1 Cor. 7:23)
To think that he hung dying there while soldiers rolled their dice.   (John 19:24)

His final thought was to forgive; with all that he went through,
He asked his father to forgive, they know not what they do.   (Luke 23:34)
And even when his side was pierced, another sacrifice,   (John 19:34)
He found a way to bring a thief with him to Paradise.   (Luke 23:43)

They offered him some vinegar and gall for him to drink,   (Matt. 27:34)
But Jesus would not drink it, so his mind could clearly think.
For Jesus knew the prophecies and everything at stake.   (Ps. 69:21)
So even though he thirsted much, he chose not to partake.   (John 19:28)

I couldn't begin to understand how deep God's love could be,   (Eph. 3:18)
Until I saw his mercy flow while he bled on that tree.
He let himself endure all this and die so I might live.
No greater gift, no bigger price could my Lord ever give.   (1 Pet. 1:18)

Another thing that makes me know the depth of what took place
Was the separation Jesus felt when sin blocked out God's face.
The Trinity was ripped apart; our sin had caused the rift.
He thought God had abandoned him, although he was God's gift.   (Matt. 27:46; Mark 15:34)

All of Hades thought God lost; they all began to cheer.
What were the odds that they would see a risen Lord appear?
For Satan thought the cross would be the scene where he would win.
He did not see that God had planned to cleanse us from our sin.

For when Christ died and went below, what happened next is key.
For Jesus went to Satan's throne and set the captives free.
He took the keys for death itself, their kingdom ripped to shreds.   (Rev. 1:18)
All of Hades now in shock, they must have scratched their heads.

For God had planned it long before; it was no accident.
The cross is more than just a fight; it was the main event.
The story of the cross is more than how my Savior died,
It showed how Satan could not win, no matter how he tried.

So now when I think of the cross, I have a different view.
It speaks to me of promises that Jesus made come true.
Our Lord had died so we could find atonement for our sin.   (Ps. 79:9)
No matter what we face in life, with God we always win.   (Ps. 44:7; 1 Cor. 15:57)

Staying the Course

I think the hardest thing we face is waiting to see change.
Sometimes we try to stretch our faith but seem to lack the range.
For often when we start to pray, we're confident and keen,
But over time, hope starts to fail when changes can't be seen.

The battle that we start to face is in the spiritual realm.
So keep your hope in God who reigns, he's always at the helm. (Ps. 47:8)
For you must know we face a foe who tries to make us fail.
He whispers things and tells us lies so our faith starts to flail. (John 8:44)

We must have trust that God's got this, he rules eternity.
And that is why we cannot lean on what we know and see. (Prov. 3:5)
He is the God that goes before us to make our path go straight. (Deut. 1:30)
The problem that we often face is we don't want to wait.

We try to figure it all out and tell God when and how.
And as for when it should occur, we want it done right now.
But God sees more than we can see; he always sees it through.
You need to trust in God alone and know his Word is true.

Praise and worship are keys to staying true to course.
And don't let guilt and shame stop you, just hold tight to the source.
Satan lies and makes us think we don't deserve God's best.
He makes us feel unworthy, and we need to pass this test.

We need to use God's promises to tell our foe he's wrong.
We need to have God's armor on so our faith can stay strong. (Eph. 6:11)
Addictions can be tough to break, a weakness we have made,
Remember this is why Christ died, part of the price he paid. (Rom. 4:7)

He is the God who rescues you, the battle is the Lord's. (1 Sam. 17:47)
His mercy, which will follow you, he graciously awards.
He frees us from our fears and doubts and frees us from our chains. (Pss. 34:4; 116:16)
Therefore, I will keep praising him, the God who truly reigns.

Yet why does it seem when we pray some problems just get worse?
You'd think that when we call on God, the issue would reverse.
Compare this to a rose that's cut, which looks like it's alive.
But it's been cut off from its source, so it will not survive.

Much like a rose, after we pray, our problems seem intact.
We cannot see what God has done; we think he did not act.
The problem is our battle is not only flesh and blood.
Our God is breaking bondages, he comes in like a flood.   (2 Sam. 5:20)

The rose can still begin to bloom right before our eyes.
Our problems sometimes do this, too, before they vaporize.
So stay the course when there's no change; you simply do not see
That God is fighting on your side to get the victory.   (1 Chron 22:18)

I wonder why I always look for ways to not trust God.
It seems I cannot trust myself, my thinking is so flawed.   (1 Cor. 14:20)
It doesn't help when those around can add to my own doubt.
You'd think that family would support, but often they bail out.

For only you can know what God has put into your heart.   (Luke 16:15)
So trust in him, he will not fail, he always does his part.
Just listen to his still small voice, he'll show you where to go.
And as you see him meet your needs, your faith will surely grow.

Remember All He's Done
(Lest I Forget)

Unwavering faith's a tricky thing; it's hard to keep in place.   (Heb. 10:22, 23)
So many things can distract me with all the trials I face.
I need to look at where I've come and what my God has done,   (Deut. 10:21)
Interceding on my behalf with favor from his Son.

It's easy to see what went wrong and focus on the bad,
When I should see his promises, which help my heart stay glad.
The Word is full of promises that God has made for me.
My mind should dwell on good reports, his promises are key.

The times when I thought I would fail and had no hope at all,   (Ps. 74:20)
My Savior reached into my life and made the final call.   (Ps. 144:2)
He is the God who goes before when life becomes a storm.
The times when I have zero strength are when he will perform.

His promises will be fulfilled; they're always proven true.   (2 Sam. 22:31; Ps. 18:30)
They are my shield, my best defense, they help me make it through.   (Ps. 144:2)
His hope will let me stay secure and help my mind to cope,
So courage will rise up in me; it's brought about by hope.   (Job 11:18)

I often doubt because I fail to recognize his hand
When God was there to keep me safe against what Satan planned.   (Ps. 121:3)
The miracles I didn't see, that suddenly appeared,
A problem, pain, or illness that just quickly disappeared.

A lucky break, a bus that's late, a person I just met,
All these things that God planned out to wipe away a threat.
He is the God who conquers all that Satan throws my way.
I'll stay in peace, keep hope in place, and praise him every day.   (Ps. 71:22)

So think on all these precious times, look closely at the facts,
And you will see what God arranged and how his grace impacts.   (John 1:17; 4:6–8)
When times are tough and life is hard, remember all he's done.   (Ps. 66:16)
He is the rock, the quiet place, the ever-constant one.

Our faith is built on solid ground when we keep God in sight.   (Ps. 119:140)
That is why I think on times when God has joined my fight.
So many times he kept close watch when I was in distress,   (Ps. 121:7)
And even when I failed his test, he helped clean up my mess.

How can I doubt a God who knows the future and the past,   (Rev. 1:8; Ps. 90:2)
Who gives me strength to carry on when my own strength won't last?
I trust in God who loves me so and wants for me the best.   (John 16:7)
I'll work to be obedient and let him do the rest.   (Dan. 9:4)

My hope stays fixed in knowing that my God can never fail.   (Heb. 13:5)
No matter what life throws at me, his promises avail.
So when a trial or trouble mounts, I will not be afraid.
I'll remember what God has done, so my hope will not fade.   (Rom. 4:21)

Beauty for Ashes

I think of Job and what he faced when he was serving God.
He seemed to live a godly life, yet still his heart was flawed.
I seem to face this problem, too, and sometimes I wonder why
The problems seem to always come the harder that I try.

At times I worry—will one day I finally meet my end,
And because I didn't do enough, my God I did offend.
But then I think about his Word, the promises within,
I realize the devil tries to make my faith grow thin.

He wants me to feel weak, or worse, he wants me to give up.
He knows if I dwell long enough, the guilt will soon build up.
The Bible makes a promise that I use to conquer fear.
Isaiah spoke this promise, which my heart hears loud and clear.

He promises to give to me beauty for my ashes. (Isa. 61:3)
He takes my pain and brings me joy so often when life crashes.
He tells me that no matter what, he's there to help me through.
And I believe the Word of God, his promises are true.

The Word tells us to worship him and sing in accord.
And praise the beauty of the One who is our holy Lord. (2 Chron. 20:21)
His holiness, beauty fulfilled, I get once I am saved,
To take away the times when sin has kept my life enslaved.

He takes my failures and my pain and washes them away.
His oil of joy replaces times when mourning comes my way.
Like Job, I will not let bad breaks define where I will go.
I'll keep my faith in God above and watch his blessings flow.

One key to letting beauty come is to throw away the ash.
Release the guilt when you mess up; throw out this useless trash.
When you do not forgive yourself, peace cannot stay inside.
For joy cannot fill up our hearts if grief and pain reside.

The ash can stay for many years if we still cling to it.
Cast all of it at Jesus's feet, and to his will submit.
The garment of his praise can help restore your heart and mind,
And that is when his beauty comes; it is a precious find.

For when our hearts and minds release the guilt, the shame, the blame,
Then we can focus on our God and happiness reclaim.
But unforgiveness blocks our way and keeps the ash around,   (Matt. 6:15)
So quickly learn to let it go so favor can be found.

Then you can be his instrument, a tree of righteousness.
Then peace and joy can be restored, replacing your distress.
Where beauty shines, the ash is gone, so you can move toward
Isaiah's words, where you are called "a planting of the Lord."   (Isa. 61:3)

The God Who Rescues Us

I saw a sticker on a car that told me Jesus saves.
It's a fact that most ignore this phrase, despite what each man craves.
The world is lost and seeks a way to find security.
But most don't look beyond today to their eternity.

Their eyes are blinded to the fact our spirit will endure.
So they don't look to find the truth, to keep their life secure.
The world tells them there is no truth, just what you can perceive,
The devil's lie to fool humankind, a tactic to deceive.

But I know that my Lord saved me; it's not some fairy tale.
I need no quest to save my soul for Christ is my holy grail.
Only Jesus can save me—the life, the truth, the Way.   (John 14:6)
And when I take him as my Lord, my sins are washed away.   (Acts 22:16)

But there is more we need to see; salvation means much more.
So many ways he rescues us, and these truths we can't ignore.
He is the God who rescues us from the trials we face each day.   (Ps. 37:40)
Some trials he helps us battle through, while some he takes away.

Sometimes we face a mountain where the climb looks way too steep.
Sometimes we feel we're on a ledge, afraid to take a leap.
Trust God to give you his own strength to help you reach the peak.
He is the God who rescues us, no chasm is too deep.

We need to know when we ask God to answer all our prayers,
That he knows what is best for us; he is the God who cares.
Sometimes the answer will be no; trust God, and you'll stay strong.
Sometimes the door will close on us so our path won't go wrong.

Just like the Word, which tells us not to fear when times look tough,
Jehovah Jireh, never fails, our God who is enough.   (Gen. 22:14; 1 John 4:9)
So worry not when troubles mount, our God is in control.
Sometimes the trials are in our lives to help us reach his goal.

Sometimes they're there to stretch our faith so it can have more range.   (James 1:2)
Sometimes they're there to do a work in us so we can change.
Sometimes he shows out in our life when odds seem way too slim,
So people know it's not by us, the glory goes to him.

The basic truth is we cannot know how our God does all,   (Prov. 3:5)
And that is why we cannot fret when progress seems to stall.
Just think of Joseph and his dream of what God planned for him.   (Gen. 37:5–9)
He had his brothers cast him down and then sell him on a whim.   (Gen. 37:27)

For Joseph faced so many things before his dream came true.
Falsely accused then thrown in jail, does this make sense to you?
Sold as a slave by family does not make sense to most.
But God's plan brought him to a place, that country's highest post.

God rescued him for faithfulness, despite what had transpired.
He did his best to follow God and did what God required.
If this had happened in our lives, would we still trust in God?
Or would we doubt he really cared and think his promise flawed?

The key to this is trust in God, who makes our paths go straight.   (Isa. 42:16)
Just trust that he will answer prayers, though sometimes we must wait.
The ever-present friend of ours, the rock to which we're tied,   (Ps. 18:2)
He is the God who rescues us, he's always at our side.   (Isa. 49:26)

The God Who Leads

It's funny how we look at life and think we need to know
everything that God has planned and what he wants to show.
That somehow we know what is best, the path that we should take,
When every time we take this route, we make a huge mistake.   (2 Cor. 11:30)

So how do we start out each day? What choice will help us most?
The answer is to seek our God helped by the Holy Ghost.   (Matt. 6:33)
Our lives should be so spirit-led that we know where to go.   (1 Cor. 2:11)
But we must wait for God's advice, although it could be no.

We listen for his Word each day so we don't go off track.   (John 10:4)
We walk the path that God has laid, safe from our foe's attack.   (Deut. 9:3)
We start each day with God's own plan to help us through the day.
It takes the pressure off our backs since he directs our way.   (Matt. 11:29–30)

The Bible says to seek him first; it's really for the best.
Just listen and then go work his plan, he'll take care of the rest.
It's not our job to strategize; the battle is the Lord's.
Do not fear what you'll have to face, with God we carry swords.

Our life is like a mountain trek, where God's our Sherpa guide,
Jesus paid the price for it, and we are well supplied.
When on this climb, we're not to lead but follow where we're led.   (2 Cor. 2:14)
But we don't like to follow when we can't see what's ahead.

So many choose to go in front, to direct God instead.
Yet God, the guide, knows everything; he knows where we should tread.
He has the knowledge that we need, and he knows what is in store.
So why do we think we can lead the God who goes before?   (Deut. 1:30)

Our life can be a mountain storm, we're blinded as we walk.
And that is why we must seek God's directions when we talk.
Stay close to him; his threefold cord will keep you safe from harm.   (Eccles. 4:12)
His mighty wings will block life's winds, you're safe under his arm.

It makes me shake my head sometimes at how we are so blind.
Our burdens should be cast on him, they should be left behind.
The Sherpa doesn't make the person carry all the gear.
So why do we keep trudging forth with guilt, shame, and fear?   (Deut. 2:7)

He is the answer we all need when we just drift around.
We do not stop to think that God can keep us on safe ground.   (Deut. 31:8)
The Bible says that we are fools when we think we are smart.
Wisdom comes from God alone, just listen with your heart.

So do not lean on what you know, let God direct your path.   (Prov. 3:5)
For when we lead we make a mess, a painful aftermath.
So start each morn, sit quietly, and listen when you pray.
A simple word can do so much to help improve your day.   (Luke 12:12)

Poem Journal: God's Inspiration:

WEEK 55

The Lighthouse

We're like a ship tossed to-and-fro, caught in a raging storm.
Our life gets rocked when we steer it, so much it seems the norm.
The trouble comes in like a fog, and we can't see our way,   (Ps. 40:12)
So therefore we must seek the Lord to guide us every day.   (Exod. 15:13)

For when I choose to steer the boat, those times I oft regret.
Since God has charted out my life, he knows what course to set.   (2 Sam. 22:33)
Why do I fight to take control? I sail right for the reef!
If not for his unfailing grace, I'd find more pain and grief.

For when we search for God above, he says he can be found.
He is the light that pierces through, so we don't run aground.
So focus on his shining light, so he can guide your way.
He'll keep you safe from hidden reefs, just seek his light each day.

We fix our gaze on him alone, not on the storm around.
He is the God who goes before to keep us safe and sound.   (Isa. 26:7)
His light that shines is full of strength, the spectrum of his love.
It's more than colors we can see, it's traits of God above.

Our eyes see greens and reds and blues; his light has so much more.
It comes inside our hearts and stays, his spirit we can store.
This light can make our darkness flee; it chases out the fear.   (2 Tim 1:7)
So let his light come deep inside, despair will disappear.

His light brings joy and peace and hope, his gifts he gives to you.
And when his Spirit comes inside, it brings redemption too.
He is the light unto the world, his light brings truth and life.   (John 8:12; 14:6)
So seek it out and steer your boat away from sin and strife.

God is the lighthouse we all need so we stay true to course.
Lean not on what your mind tells you; let his light be your source.   (Prov. 3:5)
For only God, knows where to go—our compass does not work—
It always sends us down a path where rocks and shallows lurk.

Let God control when your boat sails; he knows where you should go.

Open the eyes he put inside, and let his Spirit flow. (Acts 26:18)

Then you can unfurl all your sails and live life at its best

When you seek out his light each day, and let God do the rest.

For God so Loved

We all have heard the scripture verse, "for God so loved the world."   (John 3:16)
Today it played inside my mind, inside my brain it swirled.
"For God so loved," kept playing loud; I asked God what this meant.
He told me that those first four words are why his Son was sent.

He told me to investigate, dig deeper than before.
And when I dove into his Word, I found there's so much more.
It lets us know he is a God whose love will seek us out.
"For God so loved," a central theme, explains what God's about.

I think I never fully knew how deep his love had run
Since I had never sacrificed my one and only son.
I understood about his pain, to that I could relate.
But understanding all his love, I didn't share that trait.

The fullness of his love was more than I could comprehend
How he could be so full of love, be closer than a friend.
For my love always had been tinged with pride and fear and doubt.
I never really understood that kind of love poured out.

The Bible shows us many times how God's love was extreme.
I read those tales and wondered if I was caught in a dream.
I always knew that God was love yet did not know how deep.
I finally saw how far he went; it made me want to weep.

When Jonah tried to run from God, his plan was doomed to fail.
But God's mercy went the extra mile to save him with a whale.   (Jon. 1:17)
When Balaam tried to curse the Jews, a donkey made him stop.   (Deut. 23:5)
God could have let poor Balaam die, a mighty angel's chop.

God showed his love through mercy's eyes, and this applies today.
So many times he keeps us safe when we choose our own way.
For only God would choose to save such stubborn, selfish fools
and even use the animals as his redeeming tools.

The next way we can see his love is through how redemption works.
For God adopted all of us, we got the family perks.   (1 Thess. 1:4)
He takes the lost, the sick, and the blind and helps them all to see   (Ps. 3:3)
That by his love they can be saved; his grace will set them free.

He gives us gifts we did not earn; eternal life is one.
He also let his Spirit stay, a gift from his own Son.   (Rom. 5:5)
His love is more than we deserved; it's why he is so great.
It is a gift we cannot buy; no works could pay the rate.   (Eph. 2:9)

The Bible says he first loved us, a point he wants to teach.   (1 Josh. 4:19)
Adopting us has shown to me how far his love can reach.
A choice to love no matter what, that's why he is my King.   (Eph. 1:4)
A God who seeks relationship is such a special thing.

He knew we needed to be saved; he knew the mess we'd make.
He is a God who loves us so and never would forsake.
His Son was sent to fix the gap when we had fallen short.   (Rom. 3:23)
He died and handed out to us a heaven-stamped passport.   (Eph. 5:2)

Because his love is so profound, it lets us love like him.   (1 John 4:11)
He is the model we can use when our love seems so dim.
Just think of all the things you've done, the times when you have failed,
And realize we have a God whose love can't be derailed.

There is no place his love can't reach, no matter what we've done.   (Ps. 36:5)
His love forgives and cancels guilt, it cannot be outrun.
So thank the Lord, who loved you first, then sing his praises loud.   (Ps. 66:8)
His love is patient, his love is kind, his love is never proud.   (1 Cor. 13:4)

God, let me understand right now how wide, how long, how deep   (Eph. 3:18)
your love can manifest in me and all you call your sheep.   (1 John 4:12)
It cannot fail, it gives us hope, and endures forever more.   (2 Chron. 20:21)
It lets me put my trust in you, my faith it does restore.   (Gal. 2:20)

I've only scratched the surface here; there's so much more to tell.
So many times he's proven why his praises I must yell.   (Ps. 66:1)
He heals the sick, redeems the lost, restores the weary soul.   (Jer. 31:25)
No matter how we go off course, he's always in control.

His love surrounds when we trust him and makes our hearts be glad.   (Ps. 32:10)
He is the friend who stays with us, the most amazing dad.
So when I hear, "For God so loved," my heart will hold on tight
To how he saved a wretch like me, now pleasing in his sight.   (Gal. 1:15)

Abide in Me

The Bible says, "abide in me and I'll abide in you."   (John 15:7)
The key to living in his will, it's what I need to do.
The Word says pray unceasingly, just talk to him all day.
For when you do this simple thing, much fruit you will display.

He is the vine, we are a branch, we won't find another.   (John 15:4)
He is the friend that I talk to, closer than a brother.   (Prov. 18:24)
Abiding doesn't have to be just time with him alone.
It's also casual time with him, like talking on the phone.

Just speak to him throughout the day and ask for his advice.   (James 1:5)
For when we put him first all day, we never roll the dice.
But when we do things in our strength, they can go good or bad.
Yet grace and favor follow us when talking to our dad.   (Rom. 5:2)

It seems a simple thing to do, just keep him close at hand,
So why do I still do most things by what I understand?
And why is this so hard for me to keep him top of mind?
Since when I let him in my life, his blessings I will find.

Abiding is a choice you make, put God before yourself.   (1 Cor. 7:24)
Let futile things you want to do get put up on a shelf.
Distractions come when you seek God to put him first all day.   (1 Cor. 7:35)
You must let God renew your mind every time you pray.   (Rom. 12:2)

The world can cause us not to pray when troubles do draw near.
So focus on the prince of peace, he will remove your fear.   (Isa. 9:6)
Like Peter stepping from the boat, just fix your eyes on him.   (Matt. 14:29)
Think about your God all day, so you won't have to swim.

Then you can rise above the fear and don't begin to sink,   (Matt. 14:30)
It tends to happen at those times, we try to overthink.
We dwell on what is going wrong, not on who's in control.   (Dan. 5:23)
Abide in him, he goes before to help us reach our goal.

God works to make our paths go straight, just like a GPS.   (Prov. 11:5)
He sees the road that we will take, so we don't have to guess.
Rerouting so we don't get lost, he has the final say.
He knows the landscape of our lives, so we don't lose our way.   (1 Sam. 2:3)

One final note that must be told is how we stay on track.
Expect when you abide with God, the devil will attack.   (1 Pet. 5:8)
Be diligent to not let this deter you from your goal.   (Eph. 4:27)
Abide with God, seek out his will, and your faith can be whole.

In This Storm

I close my eyes and see my world and think I'm in a storm.
So many people feel stressed, anxiety the norm.
The rain is falling on this world, no matter who you are.   (Matt. 5:45)
No person can escape from it, from pope to movie star.

The Bible speaks of times like these, when storms rage all about.
The key is where your hope is placed to battle fear and doubt.   (Isa. 20:5; Lam. 3:24)
We need to place our hope in God for only he alone   (Ps. 119:114)
Can give us the strength that we must have; he is our cornerstone.   (Matt. 21:42; Acts 4:11)

The Bible talks about two men who build their house on land.
One builds his house upon a rock, the other chooses sand.   (Matt. 7:24–27)
God is the rock on which we build the house that is our life.
Or we can choose the shifting sand and bring on pain and strife.   (Matt. 7:26)

Upon the rock, which is our God, we can withstand the storm,   (Matt. 7:25)
And every time we talk with God, another brick we form.
Eventually we build a house where we are not alone.
For when we walk with God each day, it's like we add a stone.

But those who do not know the Lord can only build on sand.
And when the rain comes like a flood, their house will fail to stand.   (Matt. 7:27)
Without the rock they have no base to save them from the rain.
So when the flood comes surging in, their life can't take the strain.

How many people in this storm feel beaten by the wind?
With the daily drenching of bad news, their minds feel trapped or pinned.
They have no Savior to cling to, to help their hope renew.
They wander lost amid the storm, not sure they'll make it through.

The storm is often in our minds, as thoughts we must control.   (Ps. 26:2; 19:14)
We must renew our minds each day, so our house remains whole.
The devil tries to shake our house and take our strength away.
So we must seek to build it up, protect it when we pray.   (Matt. 26:41)

In every battle, God gives us the strength to make it through.   (Isa. 40:29)
So cling fast to his promises; believe that they are true.
Proclaim his Word, declare his works; let your mind be infilled.   (Ps. 73:28)
Abide in him, seek out his will, a strong house you will build.

Just look around, and you will see how most are built on sand.
These people need to come to Christ, they need a helping hand.
Some folks seem weak, others annoyed, they curse and fight and blame.
But in the end, without the Lord, their fate is all the same.

Thus, I will keep God close to me, and I'll stay on the rock.   (2 Sam. 22:47)
And when the enemy attacks, his flood I'll always block.
I'll praise the God who is our rock, not focus on the rain,   (Ps. 18:46)
For God controls the weather, too, so my house will remain.

A Closed Door

I find that I don't like to change; I like things as they are.
Yet sometimes God can't help me grow when I won't raise the bar.
Sometimes I seek out things in life that aren't the best for me.
They satisfy my flesh short term but hurt me spiritually.　　　　　(Gal. 5:13)

The hardest thing to understand is why doors close on me.
Most times I do not realize that God must prune my tree.
God is the vine, we are the branch, he wants me to bear fruit.　　(John 15:4)
But that won't happen; when I'm stuck, bad habits won't uproot.　　(Rom. 7:18)

Not every door is closed by God; I do some on my own.
Sometimes I fail to heed his voice, and advancement I have blown.
Sometimes I let the devil steal what God has planned for me,　　(Prov. 4:23)
Not trusting what the Lord has said, fooled by the enemy.　　(2 Pet. 3:17)

Sometimes when doors are slammed on me, it cuts me like a knife,
When friends and family walk away, no longer in my life.
The devil throws this in my face, so I feel guilt and shame.
I listen to his blatant lies and justify his blame.　　(John 8:44)

I second-guess what I have chosen, decisions I have made.
That somehow it is all my fault, a price that I have paid.
But this is how the devil works, accusing us each day,
So we sit down and blame ourselves, and in that spot we stay.

We focus on the guilt and shame when God has all the keys.
And God can open any door, he opens them with ease.　　(Rev. 3:8)
So when a door seems locked to you, you need to stop and pray.
And ask the Lord, who sees it all, if it should stay that way.

Sometimes we think a door is best when God sees it as wrong.
So you can't force it open when God closed it all along.　　(2 Thess. 3:3)
God often will close doors on us to keep us from more pain,　　(Ps. 121:7)
And he will open other doors, so blessings we can gain.

So never see a door that's locked as permanent at all.
God may have closed it for a while; he has the final call.
The timing may be wrong right now, he knows what's best for you,   (Eph. 1:11)
So lean on him and trust his will, and he will see you through.

Remember that he is a God who sees the paths we make.
He loves you and protects his own from paths they shouldn't take.   (Ps. 97:10)
He knows our foe lies waiting and sets off an alarm.
So realize that God moves us to keep us from some harm.   (Prov. 19:23)

So if a door is closed on you, stay focused on the Lord.
And pray to him for guidance so your vision is restored.
For only God knows what you need; ignore the devil's lies.
You never know when locked doors are a blessing in disguise.

❧ WEEK 60

Perspective

One lesson that I finally learned is God knows more than me.
When I am facing anything, look at it biblically.
It teaches what to focus on, it puts things in their place,
So our perspective is correct with every trial we face.

When you face giants in a fight, where does your focus lie,
With odds on whether you should win or God who rules on high?
Both Abraham and Sarah knew; God promised them a son.   (Gen. 17:19)
When looking at this logically, the chance of this was none.

But Abraham ignored the facts and trusted in the Lord.   (Rom. 4:18)
He held God's promise close to him, his weakness he ignored.
His faith sustained him through the doubt that God would keep his Word,
When all the time his mind told him to think this is absurd.

But in the end it came to pass, God's promise did come true.   (Gen. 21:5)
When God says something to your heart, let faith sustain you too.
Do we believe what God has said, what he puts in our heart?
Or do we let the doubt creep in and tear our faith apart.

Do we trust what the world tells us? We listen to the news,
Or do we go to God with things? Which one do you most choose?
We must hold fast the Bible's truths, keep hope and faith intact.   (Ps. 119:31)
And not let fear and doubt rule us in how we think or act.

It's not that we ignore all facts; our faith should not be blind.
But there are times when we've heard God and must keep that in mind.
It's whether our perspective is on problems or on God.
For when we only see the trial, our perspective is flawed.

We need to pray and meditate and listen to his voice.   (John 10:3; Deut. 30:20)
For only then we have the facts, we make a proper choice.
The crooked path is always there; the Bible says that so.
But God can straighten it for you so you know where to go.   (Prov. 21:8)

I think of when Elisha faced an army all around.
His servant went outside in shock; he saw what did surround.   (2 Kings 6:15–17)
When he cried out, Elisha said you needn't be afraid.
Open your eyes, and look again, and you will see our aid.

God let him see what men can't see, his eyes were opened wider,
He saw an army on the hills with chariots of fire.   (2 Kings 6:17)
When you think trials surround your life, remember God above.
He will surround what surrounds us and protects with his love.

We must heed both our common sense and promises from God.
But if we only look at facts, our insight won't be broad.
Faith's the substance of things not seen, we must seek him each day,
For even when the world says no, God has the final say.   (Rom. 13:1)

A Blessing from the Lord

The key to moving forward now is looking where we went.
The last year was a trying time, a strange and odd event.
It started as a normal year, but then things went south so quick
As people started panicking, worried they'd get sick.

If I could pick a word that fits to describe what I feel,
I would pick "stuck," for many felt that it did not feel real.
Many people just put on hold the things that they would do.
While others smiled when they found out their kids just had the flu.

I think we must all look at this as part of God's great plan.
It started letting many see the folly that is man.
The fighting, yelling, bickering, the fear and hate stirred up.
It showed me that without our God, our wisdom won't hold up.   (Heb. 12:15)

So many took their eyes away from God who runs it all,
To worry that their social life was simply going to stall.
Our rights and feelings took the stage, with fear and doubt in charge.
And many people felt burnt out, with no plug to recharge.

I think we need to change our view and focus on the Lord.
Put on the armor he provides and bring with us his sword.   (Eph. 6:13)
Remember who we represent, and focus on his Word.
And listen close to what he says, and keep our spirits stirred.   (Heb. 10:24)

It's like when Moses took the Jews toward the Promised Land,
With many people so confused while trudging through the sand.
It was a journey I would say that never made progress,
Like waiting for another move when in a game of chess.

To get them to the Promised Land, think about what our God has done.
He parted seas and brought them food, the battles that they won.
When on the journey, God himself told Moses how to bless.   (Num. 6:22)
When reading it, it made me think, *It's what we should confess.*

The blessing showed the character of God, who was their guide.
He protected them and kept them safe, the manna he supplied.   (Exod. 16:35)
The blessings speak of actions that our God will do for you,
And understanding all of these will help you make it through.

It starts with telling us that God will bless and protect you.   (Num. 6:24)
This tells us that he is our source, a fact we know is true.
While on our journey we need God to help our paths stay straight,   (Isa. 45:2)
A friend who always stays with us, to help us navigate.

It also says he smiles at you, and his grace will follow too.   (Num. 6:25)
This lets us know he wants the best of things for me and you.
May the Lord show you his favor, and give you all his peace.   (Num. 6:26)
This means that we can stay relaxed while blessings he'll release.

This illustrates for all of us what God will do for those
Who love the Lord, who rules it all, his people that he chose.
So choose to bless and not to stress; God loves and protects you.
And when you bless, it also says, that he will bless you too.   (Num. 6:27)

That is my wish for twenty-one, that hope returns to all.
That people see how great God is and start to heed his call.
Then understand the peace he brings, the fear he can remove,
And know that your God walks with you, and your life he will improve.

My Psalm

Sometimes I feel like David when he cried out to the Lord.
When troubles seemed too much for him, his fear and tension soared.
But shouldn't I be better off as God's spirit is inside?   (Acts 2:38)
And don't I have his strength within because my Savior died?

Yet times when I feel weak and drained and know what I should do,
I watch myself sit powerless, worn out, and feeling blue.
I love my God, like David did, and want to do his will.
But sometimes I feel stuck in the mud while climbing up a hill.

As David also prayed to God to keep him safe from harm,
We can use our faith as well; it's not some lucky charm.
Yet why do I allow myself to sit and feel so stressed,
When if I really look at things, I see how I've been blessed?

The answer lies within God's Word; just look and you will see
That even though Christ is with us, we face the enemy.   (1 Pet. 5:8)
The enemy attacks the church while seeking to devour.
That is why we need God's strength, his joy, his peace, his power.

This poem is a psalm for me, like ones that David wrote,
To show me what my God can do and why I shouldn't gloat.
For only God can give me strength, he hears me when I pray,
So I can stand, then stand some more, in battles every day.   (1 Cor. 16:13)

We all must do our parts as well; we can't just sit and wait.
We must get up like batters do and walk up to the plate.
We do not have, if we don't ask, his promises that are true.   (2 Sam. 22:31)
So boldly trust that God will give what he has promised you.

Then David chose to praise his God, declaring all his deeds,
Proclaiming how his Lord is great by meeting all his needs.   (Ps. 35:28)
So, we can do, what David did, and praise God every day,   (Ps. 145:2)
Recalling all his miracles and how he led our way.   (Ps. 143:5)

He told us how God's enemies are scattered in defeat,   (Ps. 89:10)
And how the Lord can comfort us if we just leave cares at his feet.   (1 Pet. 5:7)
But we must take this step of faith and trust God will protect.
Only God knows what will come; his plans he will perfect.   (Isa. 25:1)

We use our faith before we see the promises fulfilled.   (Heb. 11:1)
He is the God who calms the storms, the waters he has stilled.   (Luke 8:24)
Is anything too hard for God, who rules the universe?   (Jer. 32:17, 27)
So don't let Satan steal your hope and think things will get worse.

The world around can run amok, in chaos and defeat,
But I will look only to God, who never can be beat.   (Ps. 123:2)
And like a psalm I write these words as he inspires me.
For no one else comes close to him, his face I long to see.   (Ps. 86:8)

Our God Reigns

With everything I see today, emotions can erupt.
I take my focus off my God, and my thoughts become corrupt.
I listen to the enemy, and fearful thoughts begin.
Then in my mind, I visualize how chaos will set in.

I need to know that my God reigns, so faith can push fear out,   (Ps. 118:6)
And only faith can give me peace when my path seems in doubt.   (Prov. 1:33)
So why does my mind visualize the worst scenario?
When reality is not so bleak, God shows me where to go.

How often do I look at life and think I've dug a hole,
Thinking my past imprisons me for life, with no parole?
I think that God is sitting there in judgment and upset,
When his love sent his Son to die and fully paid my debt.

Tests and trials will come my way, no matter how I live,
So I must stand and overcome with strength he'll always give.   (Isa. 40:29, 31)
I serve a God who's always near, he's always in control,   (Ps. 103:19)
His promises are always true, his love I will extol.   (Ps. 18:30)

He chooses paths I would not think or dream that I could go.
So I must choose to trust in him as my future he does know.
I must believe his promises will keep me safe from harm,
And any traps that Satan sets, God's ready to disarm.

Remember we've been set apart, redeemed by God's own Son.   (Acts 26:18)
We're sheltered underneath his wings; we serve the mighty one.   (Ruth 2:12)
No weapon formed against us can defeat us if we know   (Isa. 54:17)
We serve the God who rules it all, he's conquered every foe.   (Rev. 17:14)

So when I look around the world and see what's going on,
I realize God's in control, each ruler is his pawn.   (Prov. 8:15)
I simply need to trust in him, though his plans I cannot grasp.
And if he lets me see his plans, I think that I would gasp.

For knowing that God's on the throne will take away my doubt,   (Rev. 19:6)
And nothing is too big for God, I trust he will win out.   (Jer. 32:17)
He rules it all, omnipotent, controls all government,   (Dan. 7:14)
And any plans that God has made, he's sure to implement.

God sits upon his holy throne, clothed in his majesty.   (Ps. 93:1)
Removing chains like sin and shame, his Son has set me free.   (John 8:36)
I will rejoice and tell the world my Savior reigns supreme.   (1 Chron. 16:31)
It doesn't matter who I face, he's conquered every scheme.

Peace and joy have filled my heart for God has got my back.
And every day he walks with me and keeps my life on track.
I wait on him, expectantly, for what he has in store.   (Ps. 5:3)
I praise and glorify his name, he reigns forevermore.   (Rev. 1:18)

Pit Stops

A memory flashed within my mind of when I saw a race,
With cars that sped around a track at such a frantic pace.
Each driver had a plan to win, to break out from the pack.
Some started at the pole up front while others from the back.

The part I really liked to watch was when they changed out tires.
The pit crews moved in harmony, the ultimate suppliers.
For if they failed to get things done, the car could lose its place.
Efficiency was what they showed to help them win the race.

Our life is like a race we're in for God we must make room.   (Heb. 12:1)
The finish line for all of man, salvation or their doom.   (1 Cor. 9:24)
Our life will have its ups and downs, with valleys and with peaks.
At some point, we will hit the pits, and it's there we make the tweaks.

Satan tells us we're no good, that we should just stay there,
We're never going to win the race; we haven't got a prayer.
The key is do we race alone, or do we have a crew?
For in the pits we win or lose, the choice is up to you.

The Bible says to seek fellowship to help us run the race   (2 Cor. 8:4)
For when we have a crew with us, protection we embrace.
When two or more go through the course, the Lord can guide our route. (Matt. 18:20)
The obstacles cannot stop us when we display God's fruit.

We all face times when we are weak and troubles feel so large.
Pit stops are part of all our lives when we need to recharge.
It's in these pits, when out of fuel, we often need a crew
To pray for us and help restore with all that we've been through.   (Eccles. 4:10)

When you are tired and have no strength, pit stops you don't postpone.
Don't ever think that God has planned for you to race alone.   (Heb. 13:5)
Our foe would like us to give up, to come down off the track.
He tries to make us all lose hope, it is his best attack.

For Satan knows when we're alone, he can disrupt our race.
But with a crew uplifting us, our hope will stay in place.
For when our crew unites as one in prayer against the foe,   (Ps. 133:1)
We see our fuel tank get filled up, God's spirit starts to flow.   (Eph. 4:13)

Then we can leave the pits with speed and race back on the track.
For when we're energized by God, we have no need or lack.
So pray as one, in unity, so God can make repairs.
He will renew your strength and zeal; he is the God who cares.   (Isa. 40:31)

One final thought: The Bible states that some are stopped by lies.
They listen to the wrong advice and never take the prize.   (1 Cor. 9:24)
Keep joy and peace as passengers so your faith will not lag.   (Acts 20:24)
Be vigilant, and race with care to reach the checkered flag.

Poem Journal: God's Inspiration:

WEEK 65

In the Desert

Sometimes I feel a thirst inside, one that I can't explain.
Like when I'm in the sun too long, my strength begins to wane.
People going to-and-fro, yet I feel stuck in place.
It's like my feet are in cement, while others seem to race.

It's like I have a need to pull away from everything.
I get a feeling deep inside; it is an odd feeling.
I need to be alone with God, I feel the Spirit's call,   (Mark 14:39)
The only way to quench this need is by blocking out it all.

Be still and know that I am God, will occupy my mind.   (Ps. 46:10)
I need to stop and listen close; it's how I've been designed.
There are times when God will direct us out of our comfort zone,   (1 Thess. 3:11)
And that is why we must be still to walk the path he's shown.   (Ps. 31:3)

Like Jesus who would use a boat to distance from the crowd,   (Matt. 9:1)
God takes us to a quiet place when our world gets too loud.
For only when we seek his face can we know what he sees.   (Ps. 105:4)
To understand the picture clearly, we must get on our knees.

Temptation also follows us when we seek out the Lord.   (James 1:12)
Satan often comes to us before we've been restored.   (Matt. 26:41)
He tempts our bodies, minds, and souls, seeking our defeat,
Often throwing trials at us to knock us off our feet.

But in these times when we feel weak, God's Word can make us strong.
The lies that Satan speaks to us, God's Word will prove them wrong.
First, Satan tells us we will fail, but God says we will win.
Then Satan says we are too flawed, but Jesus conquered sin.

Next Satan says we're all alone, but God stays by our side.   (Prov. 18:24)
Then Satan says that there is no sin, but God says he has lied.
Satan shows things from our past to try to tear us down.
Then Christ shows us his hands and scars and offers us his crown.

Satan tries to make us scared, but God gives us his peace,   (Isa. 9:6)
And anytime fear grips our hearts, those chains God will release.
Then Satan says that life's too hard, that we will never cope,
But Jesus says his yoke is light, and God restores our hope.

Our foe then lies and says to us, "Your kids will go astray."
But then God's Word reminds our hearts, they'll come to him one day.
For God will always be faithful and finish what he starts.   (John 4:34)
His promise says they'll serve the Lord, and he will soften their hearts.

We grow in Christ when we resist the lies that Satan spreads
And seek to gain the greatest prize, the truth his Word embeds.
We often see the biggest growth in struggles that we find,
For when we use the sword of truth, he will renew our mind.   (Rom. 12:2)

The desert often is the place where God can help us grow.
When we can't do things in our strength, before him we must go.
For only in our submission can we receive his power.
When we rely on him alone, he is our mighty tower.   (2 Sam. 22:3)

So when your path looks bleak or dry, do not let your heart sink.
For God will always rescue you and satisfy with drink.
For God is all the strength we need, the source for everything,   (Exod. 15:2)
So praise his name and thank him now and let your voices sing.

God Has a Plan

The biggest thing I struggle with is trusting in the Lord.
I fail to ask for his advice, and sometimes it's ignored.
I try to do things on my own, thinking I know best,
While God has made a plan for me, and I should stay at rest.

It's not that I don't think God can, I just don't want to wait.
I make my path go crooked when God tries to make it straight.
I think that I must do my part because I want to serve.
I fail to listen for his voice, and my path begins to swerve.

I know God should direct my path; it's written in his Word. (Ps. 37:234)
But then I do some foolish things, neglecting what I've heard.
Why can't I simply wait and rest? His timing is the best.
Instead, I try to force some things and watch it all get messed. (Prov. 20:24)

For God knows what is best for me and how my life should go.
I simply need to rest in him and let him lead the show.
I need to seek his will each day, not run on what I know.
I need to better listen when my spirit tells me whoa!

Abraham was told by God that he would have a son. (Gen. 15:4)
He used a maid to have a child, but not the promised one. (Gen. 16:2)
For this is not what God had planned, it's not what he was shown,
This goes to prove how things go bad when we act on our own.

God will fulfill his promises, they always will come true. (2 Sam. 22:31)
No man can know the ways of God, we simply have no clue,
So trust that God is in control, and seek his will each day.
Life has instructions that will work, you get them when you pray.

We need to learn to let God lead and wait to hear his voice.
Then we can step out on his Word and make the perfect choice.
God always wants the best for us and can direct our feet.
But sometimes when we need God's help, we need to take a seat.

God cannot help us in a trial if we think we're in charge.
We need to submit to his will, and then he will show up large.
The good news is that God can take a mess and make it right—
But only if we let him lead, not do things in our might.

Then God can lead us down the path that we were meant to go,
And see his promises fulfilled and see his blessings flow.
His purpose for our lives can be established in our walks,
If only we sit quietly and listen when he talks.

Lord, help me better follow you, help guide my path each day.
Teach me how to lean on you so my path will not stray.
May your words stay alive in me so my words follow you.
So I go down the path you've set; with your plan, I stay true.

Justified

There are times when I can struggle with the feelings inside me,
Especially when I feel attacked by my own family.
I feel an ache within my heart that I can't seem to shake.
It stops me from getting needed rest as I lie wide awake.

My feelings start to take control and tell me what to do.
They cause me to lash out at them before I think it through.
My feelings told me I was wrong, that I was justified,
But the source of this, if I look back, was my own selfish pride.

My heart was hardened by the pain, and anger filled my mind.
I said some things I shouldn't have, my words no longer kind.
My feelings are my jury now, my brain becomes the judge.
I feel that I am justified to hold on to this grudge.

Our careless words can do much harm when used as an attack.
They lodge in other people's hearts and can't be taken back.
Relationships take time to build, be careful what you say,
A lifetime's worth of victories can be defeated in one day.

Our unforgiveness changes us, we only think of self.
It takes the peace we feel inside and puts it on a shelf.
With unforgiveness in our hearts we play the victim role.
But in the end, it cripples us and leaves a gaping hole.

It also pushes God away; it's hard to hear his voice
When payback is prioritized and bitterness our choice.
We need to let forgiveness reign, opposing how we feel.   (Matt. 6:14)
It is the choice that we must make so we can start to heal.

The Bible says forgiveness is the path that we must take.   (Matt. 18:21)
Since unforgiveness poisons us, our souls can be at stake.   (Mark 11:26)
The Bible states that vengeance is not ours but God's alone.
So when bad words are hurled at you, do not pick up a stone.

The key is recognizing quickly that feelings will arise.
But you can use the Word of God to remedy the lies.
We need to handle hurtful words with kindness and God's love.   (2 Tim. 2:24)
And when we are attacked in life, we need to rise above.

Bitterness can wreck our lives when we do not forgive.
Staying angry at someone is not how we should live.
Being kind and patient is how God wants us to be.   (1 Cor. 13:4)
It is the fruit that we should bear, it's what the world should see.

For God will vindicate us; he knows what has occurred.   (Ps. 26:1)
He knows what others say to us as he's heard their every word.
Trust God to balance our accounts, his justice you will see,   (Isa. 35:4)
Just follow what he asks of you, so your heart can be free.

It's not about who did you wrong or justice that is due.
The price of bitterness inside is way too high for you.   (Heb. 12:15)
The chains you wear when you hold on to grudges in your heart
Will weigh you down and keep you trapped and tear your life apart.

So in the end, it comes down to the choice you need to make.
Pick peace and joy, or pain and strife, which do you want to take?
Our God chose first to forgive us and then watched as his Son died.
He could have let our sin doom us and still been justified.

If Not for Grace

There are many ways to judge our lives, and our God, he sees it all— (Gen. 16:13)
Our thoughts, our words, our actions, too, the many ways we fall.
I look at life, at my mistakes, and how it could have gone.
The many times God intervened, his grace helped me go on. (Isa. 64:4)

When my decisions caused much pain to people close to me,
Those times I walked away from God, his mercy followed me. (Ps. 23:6)
I wonder how things could have gone if God's grace wasn't there.
He watched my steps and changed my course, released me from each snare. (Pss. 40:6; 140:4)

When I was angry, blaming God, he never walked away. (Heb. 13:5)
His grace abounded in my life when I deserved to pay. (2 Tim. 1:9)
His grace and mercy go beyond all blessings I could earn.
They follow me throughout my life, at each and every turn.

I'm here today because of grace, where God wants me to be.
It helped correct the paths I took and secured my destiny. (Prov. 22:2)
I serve a God who's in control, who loves me endlessly,
Who picks me up when I fall down, and won't give up on me.

If not for grace, where would I be? a question on my mind.
I realize now how much his grace and my life intertwined. (Gal. 2:21)
I wonder now how many times God's grace has played a part
In helping me avoid a path that often I would start.

"Amazing grace, how sweet the sound," those words I had often sung,
Have shown why Christ had died for me, and on that cross he hung.
Grace is the favor God brings us when we deserve much worse.
God's Word says grace cannot be earned, no way to reimburse.

With all the grace that God has shown and mercy he has sent,
Why do I now still go astray and struggle to repent.
If not for grace I would be lost in misery and despair. (Heb. 12:15)
Yet every time I make mistakes, his grace is always there.

So I can say, "If not for grace," because of what I've seen.
When Satan's tried to finish me, God's shield has come between.
God forms a wall around my life that Satan cannot breach.
If not for grace and mercy, too, I'd stay in Satan's reach.

His grace and mercy are a hedge, surrounding me each day.   (2 Josh. 1:3)
And when I walk within God's will, they can't be moved away.
I shudder when I think of all the times I trusted me.
How often that left me exposed to face the enemy.

Like David, who had made mistakes, it comforts me to know,
No matter how I mess things up, my God will never go.
The key is moving onward when thoughts tell me to sit down.
Repent, stand up, put on my sword so I receive my crown.   (Rev. 3:1)

Power in the Blood

The world today is full of fear, anxiety, and doubt.
With media and government, there's tension all about.
It's easy to get swept away with all we hear and see,
And then forget what Christ has done, crucified for me.

We know the story of the cross and why Christ came to die.
But sometimes we still fail to grasp just what his blood would buy.
He was the sacrificial lamb, who died to save my soul,
Yet there is more his blood contained and how it makes me whole.

We need to understand the role that blood played in the past.
A spotless lamb was sacrificed, a fix that didn't last.   (Exod. 12:5)
Before the Lord had conquered sin, such offerings were made,   (Exod. 30:10)
For man had sinned, whose wage is death, a debt that must be paid.   (Heb. 10:4)

A lamb was used to cover sin, it was not washed away.   (Lev. 4:28)
But Jesus's blood did all of that on crucifixion day.
And that is why the blood of Christ means so much more to me.
His sacrifice has paid the price for all eternity.   (Heb. 7:27)

In Egypt, when the plagues appeared, when death came with a sword,
The blood was put upon the posts so that house was ignored.   (Exod. 12:23)
The blood had kept the people safe, it acted like a shield,
The angel came to kill the firstborn; the blood had made it yield.

The power of his blood protects, keeps us safe from harm,
The weapons of the enemy, it also helps disarm.   (Isa. 54:17)
So when this evil world today comes at us like a flood,
We need to claim and use the power from our own Savior's blood.

His blood has conquered death itself; he now holds all the keys.   (Rev. 1:18)
The debt that none of us could pay, his blood could now appease.
The blood has given righteousness, washed away our sins,   (1 John 1:7)
Our covenant with God renewed, like wine in new wineskins.   (Luke 5:38)

The blood of Christ renews our minds so we can serve our Lord.   (Heb. 9:14)

The blood of Christ lets us approach, relationship restored.   (Eph. 2:3)

There's healing power in his blood, from stripes upon his back,

It makes a hedge around our lives when we're under attack.

We can come to God himself, come right up to his throne,   (Heb. 10:19)

Because we serve the living God, who is our cornerstone.

The precious blood of Jesus Christ, the spotless lamb of God,

Has paid a ransom I could not because I was so flawed.   (Rom. 3:23)

My Savior's blood now covers me, I'm righteous in the Lord,

A sacrifice he made for me, his blood that freely poured.

His blood has conquered death itself, now death has lost its sting.   (1 Cor. 15:55)

So I will claim the blood of Christ, who reigns and is my King.

Passing the Test

The world today will compromise, take shortcuts where it can.
But God wants us to be our best, and that should be our plan.
The Bible shows us people who climbed higher than their fears.
Through ethics and integrity, they rose above their peers.　　　　(2 Chron. 19:7)

Their faith in God remained steadfast, no matter what they faced.
They knew that God could rescue them; it was a test they aced.
How often when we face a test does our hope disappear?
We fail to pass this test from God when we succumb to fear.

Take Joseph, who was told by God that he would rule one day.　　　　(Gen. 37:8)
You would have thought that he'd be blessed, but it did not go that way.
Thrown in a pit, sold as a slave, accused, and thrown in jail,　　　　(Gen. 37:24, 28)
God's promise looked to be a lie, yet Joseph did not fail.

Joseph could have given up, yet he stayed at his best.
He stayed the course and kept his faith, and then outshined the rest.　　　　(Gen. 39:3, 23)
His walk did not align with how his life had gone for him.
Each trial he faced seemed so unfair, his future looked so grim.

But Joseph knew this principle, the lesson God revealed,　　　　(Dan. 2:22)
To never lose his trust in God, his deliverer and shield.　　　　(Ps. 33:20)
So even though he faced setbacks, he did all that he could.
And in the end, God's promise held, and things turned out for his good.　　　　(Gen. 41:40)

The lesson that we learn from this is to always do our best.
Keep our hope in our God alone, and then we can pass his test.
Diligence and faithfulness are traits that God admires.
Integrity and excellence will guide us through the fires.　　　　(Job 2:3; Titus 2:7)

With Daniel, too, we saw these traits; he never compromised.　　　　(Dan. 1:8)
But rising up above the rest soon made him much despised.　　　　(Dan. 6:3–5)
When people see good character, their jealousy creeps in.
They are forced to look inside and wrestle with their sin.

But God is faithful to promote the ones who pass this test,   (Dan. 6:27–28)
The ones who honor what God says, and on his Word they rest.
We never know the ways of God and how things will unfold.
We simply must be good stewards and trust in what we're told.

Abraham was told by God that nations he would sire,   (Gen. 17:15)
Then later asked to sacrifice his son upon a fire.   (Gen. 22:2)
The test was his obedience, as God had planned a way,
To bring another sacrifice for Abraham that day.   (Gen. 22:11–13

So do not let both fear and doubt make hope and courage fade.
God will always bring to pass the promises he made.
The key to passing tests of faith is knowing God's our source.
God will always plan things out so our life stays on course.

Like any test, there is a chance to pass it or to fail.
You cannot simply blindly walk or you will not prevail.
The answers lie within God's Word, on Jesus's hands and feet.
So study what the Lord has done, so his grade you can meet.

Jesus is the answer to each test we'll ever face,
Knowing that he died for us, and we're saved by his grace.
So any test that you will face will not leave you perplexed.
God himself can give you the answer you need next.

The Truth

I think of when I was a child, my mum would say to me,
"You always need to tell the truth, and practice honesty."
But truth today is hard to find, deception everywhere.   (Matt. 7:13)
We reinforce our statements with, "It is the truth, I swear."

Now everything is upside down, the lies became the truth.
The world now mocks the Word of God, confusing all the youth.   (Luke 6:22)
We only need to look at where the source of lies comes from,
The serpent with the forbidden fruit, who led Eve to eat some.

Satan tries to fool humankind, sometimes with just one word.
Inclusiveness and justice now have meanings that are blurred.
The world today believes his lies and thinks they're helping man.
They go against the Word of God, it's part of Satan's plan.

Now Satan tries to tempt us all—he's looking for a crack—
Our spirits, minds, and bodies must resist his sly attack.
He even tried to twist the truth, to trick and trap the Lord.
But Jesus simply used God's Word, the Bible was his sword.

For only God can help mankind, his truth will set them free,
But Satan blinds those in his grasp; their eyes no longer see.   (2 Cor. 4:4)
Morality is now impure, with marriage now defiled.
This generation now believes that God should be exiled.

Things which used to bring us shame have now become a choice.
As people stand against God's laws, we watch the world rejoice.
The things that God said not to do, the world says yes you should.
And things that God said to avoid are advertised as good.

But I know that despite all this, the truth of God remains.
And one day God will set things right, undoing Satan's gains.   (Gal. 6:7)
Every knee will one day bow before our risen Lord,   (Rom. 14:11)
And they will see that God spoke truth, which cannot be ignored.

But those who serve him now as Lord, the ones who call him King,
Will rule with him when he returns, his kingdom he will bring.
God's truth won't change, no matter how much Satan tries to blind,   (1 John 2:11)
For in the end his truth prevails, witnessed by all mankind.

He is the truth, the way, the life, salvation is through him.   (John 14:6)
Even when the world tells lies, his truth will never dim.
So we must keep proclaiming that the Lord is truth for all,
His truth will always reign supreme, his truth will never fall.

So thank the Lord you know the truth, which cannot be denied.
Not matter what the world proclaims, we know that they have lied.
If what you hear does not align with what the Bible tells,
Just toss it in the garbage heap, it's lies that Satan sells.

Easter Message

Today we celebrate the Lord; we call this Friday good.
But when I think of what he faced, it's tough to think we should.
Today is when he died for me and hung upon a cross.
I know the reason that he died but feel his Father's loss.   (John 3:16)

I've always felt that Sunday was the day we should call good.
He conquered death and rose again, just like he said he would.   (1 Cor. 15:4)
Friday shows the price he paid; Sunday shows the gain.
Friday makes me think of all his anguish and his pain.

I know the price was higher than we all could pay alone.   (1 Pet. 2:24)
But for everything that Christ endured, we never could atone.   (1 John 4:10)
Mocked and scourged then spat upon to prove his love for me,   (Luke 18:32)
Pierced in both his hands and feet, enduring agony.   (Ps. 22:16)

Yet he stayed true to finish all his Father planned for me,
When those he came to welcome back just nailed him to a tree.   (Acts 2:23)
I find it hard to stop the tears as this scene plays in my head,
Of Jesus as the lamb of God and how his blood was shed.   (John 1:29)

I know we celebrate our King and proudly call him Lord.
But then I hear that hammer sound, which nailed him to the board.
I see the crown they made for him as thorns ripped through his skin. (Matt. 27:29)
It's hard to see this sight and think, *He suffered so I'd win.*

I picture Jesus hanging there, his blood begins to flow.
I know his blood would symbolize my sins washed white as snow.   (Isa. 1:18)
But deep inside, I cannot shake a feeling of regret
For what we made our Savior bear so he could pay our debt.   (Isa. 53:5)

His sacrifice amazes me, it shows he first loved me.   (1 John 4:19)
As God, he could have walked away, just spoke, and he'd be free.
It's one thing to go down this path for those who love you too,
Another to give up your life for those who spat on you.

Yet there are times I fail to see the total price he paid.

He conquered death and Hades, too, the cornerstone he laid. (Rev. 1:18; Ps. 118:22)

Easter is the time of year that should be number one,

The time when Christ restored our place when God gave up his Son. (1 Pet. 5:10)

God's Word is built around this theme; it all points to the cross,

When God restored relationship that long before we lost. (John 3:18)

Our Easter is when we look back at all that he has done,

The culmination of the price God paid with his own Son.

Christmas is the time of year when most think of our King.

But it was just the start of all the hope that God would bring.

Good Friday showed his sacrifice so we could be restored.

But Sunday holds the victory, for that I praise the Lord. (1 Cor. 15:57)

Spiritual Growth

I look at where I am today, my struggles and my wins,
I recognize his hand on me, forgiveness of my sins.
I see that God is now a part of every single day.
I also hear his still small voice inside me when I pray.

I used to go through life each day just knowing God was there.
But now I find myself quoting him, not only just in prayer.
He tells me that I need to read his Word to know his way.
I never thought that I would start to feel him every day.

By this I mean I look at things with eyes that know his Word.
I catch myself correcting things when wrong things I have heard.   (1 Thess. 2:4)
I criticize things on TV or things I see online
With what the Bible says to do when actions don't align.   (1 Cor. 2:13)

I simply cannot look at things the way I used to do.   (1 Tim. 4:15)
Lord, this is one effect I see from getting to know you.
I always thought that serving God would take fun things away.
Instead, I feel alive inside, his joy now fills my day.

Some things that I used to do, don't matter anymore.
As God has wiped away those thoughts, he rebooted my core.
I won't pretend that I've no sin, that I do not do wrong.
He simply helps me to resist, God helps me to be strong.

One key is speaking out the things so God can set you free.   (Titus 2:1)
For when I say them I declare his promises for me.   (Ps. 118:17)
I am strong, I must declare, even when I am weak.   (Joel 3:10)
And I can do all things through Christ, I speak throughout the week.   (Phil 4:13)

I am amazed at how often now a verse or song appears.
I sing or hum or speak it out to wipe away my fears.
I feel like God is helping me adjust the way I think.
When worry tries to take control, he causes it to shrink.

His Word's a lamp unto my feet, a light unto my path.   (Ps. 119:105)
These words cause me to feel relief, like in a bubble bath.
He is the One who goes before, he's always at my side,   (Deut. 31:8)
This is a promise God has made that brings me peace inside.

The more you dig into God's Word, the more you see his love.
The more you claim his promises, the more you let go of.   (James 4:7)
I simply know that I alone cannot change who I am.
I must surrender all to Christ for worthy is the Lamb.

Only then can real change start, can my mind be renewed.   (Rom. 12:2)
I need the power that God's Son brings so my flesh is subdued.   (1 Cor. 5:4)
I need to die to self each day and focus on his Word,   (Matt. 26:41)
Ignore the thoughts that Satan plants, and heed what I have heard.   (Luke 21:34)

The Good Book

Many people in our world think the Bible's just a book.
But there is power in God's Word if you will dare to look.
Some think God's Word is history, just stories from the past,
They do not know the Word's alive, his truth will always last.   (2 Cor. 3:3)

God's Word is more than just a book, it also is a seed.   (Luke 8:11)
When planted in the hearts of men, it grows so they are freed.
The living Word is what it is, alive forevermore.   (1 Pet. 1:23)
It is not just a simple book like others in a store.

Its truth can set the captive free, its hope restores the soul,   (Luke 4:18; Isa. 42:7)
And when you meditate on it, it makes your spirit whole.   (Ps. 119:52)
Yet many see it as a book as it gains dust on a shelf,
Not realizing that it is good medicine for self.   (Prov. 17:22)

We need to read between the lines to hear what God will say.
That is why we must declare God's Word each time we pray.
The Bible has one central theme: God's plan to save us all.   (John 3:16)
He sent his Son, a sacrifice, when mankind dropped the ball.

Many see the Bible as a guide for how to act.
But it points to eternal life and grants a spiritual pact.   (Luke 22:20)
Some people try to limit it, choose which parts to believe,
This is part of Satan's plan to blind us and deceive.

You cannot choose which parts you like and which parts to omit.   (Jer. 26:2)
Each word that's written in this book, God has inspired it.   (1 Thess. 2:13)
It is the answer sheet from God for all the tests we face.
It is the training guide we need to help us run the race.

But more than that it comes from God; it is a mighty sword   (Eph. 6:17)
That we must wield when we're attacked by Satan and his horde.
The Bible holds God's promises, which we can cling to.
Our hope and faith reside in them so we can make it through.

The Bible gives us the good news that Jesus Christ is Lord.
And when we give our life to him, our spirit is restored.
It is a book that we must read but also must be shared.   (Acts 5:42)
We live in such a messed-up world, where most are lost or scared.

No other book compares to this, their truths are mostly lies.
Ours tells of Christ who died for us and then from the grave did rise.   (Mark 16:6)
It also is a book for us that never reads the same.
God can speak so differently to those who speak his name.

A verse can give one insight into what God has planned for them,
Yet I can read that verse as well and find a different gem.
This is a book of mysteries, it's like God leaves us crumbs.
The more you read and focus on, the clearer it becomes.

Be a Joshua

God has a life designed for us with places we must go.
And there are lessons we must learn, some insights we must know.
The first is we must trust in God, and let him direct our path.   (2 Sam. 22:6)
Our understanding can be flawed, let God do all the math.   (Prov. 3:5)

One principle God teaches us is always to say, "I can."
For who can stand against our God when he has the master plan?   (2 Chron. 20:6)
Be positive and trust in him, he will not let you down.
Our Savior rules forevermore; no one can take his crown.   (Phil. 2:10)

When you feel weak say, "I am strong," it's written in his Word.   (Joel 3:10)
Declare the truth the Bible holds so your faith can be stirred.   (2 Pet. 1:13)
Your life is based on how you think, not only on what takes place.
Your attitude has great impact on how you run your race.   (1 Cor. 9:24)

Take Moses and the Israelites outside the Promised Land.
Moses sent the twelve spies in so battles could be planned.
Joshua and Caleb went and then gave a good report.   (Num. 13:30)
The other ten were filled with fear and said they should abort.   (Num. 13:31)

The two spies knew that with God's help, the battles could be won.
The other ten saw what they faced and figured they were done.   (Num. 13:33)
We need to trust God's promises, not what we've seen or heard.
The ammunition that we need is written in his Word.

The spies that felt the task too tough blamed Moses for their plight. (Num. 14:3, 4)
They felt that they would die out there, their faith was turned to fright.
Their lack of faith had displeased God, and their fears he made come true.
They never saw the Promised Land, they never made it through.   (Num. 14:22, 23)

Remember, when we face a test, to God we must submit.
No weapon formed can prosper when our God opposes it.   (Isa. 54:17)
And we can do all things through Christ, who strengthens us each day,
So you can be a Joshua and jump into the fray.

The Bible says that courage is what we must seek to find.
The biggest part is winning first the war within our mind.
God is our shield, our refuge too, he always will restore.   (Ps. 91:4; 2 Sam. 22:3)
Just follow him, and you will win; we know the final score.

God has a promised land for us, where victory is sweet.   (John 14:2)
But if we want to reach this place, we cannot speak defeat.
Like Joshua, we must be bold and ready for a fight.
The time is close—we're almost there—our promised land's in sight.

So we must think like Joshua and Caleb every day.
Know that our God is leading us and trust him when we pray.
Declare you have the victory before you go to war.
The battle is the Lord's to fight, praise God who goes before.   (2 Chron. 20:15)

The Gardener

When Jesus said, "Go tell the world," he knew how it would go.   (Acts 1:8)
Some would receive his Word with joy, while others would say no.
The heart of man has many traits, and it's these we will explore.
One scripture says that Jesus knocks, our heart is like a door.   (Rev. 3:20)

This illustrates that man must choose to open it or not.
We simply tell them why they should, salvation God has brought.   (1 Chron. 16:23)
The Bible also tells us that a heart is soft or hard.   (Job 23:16; 41:24)
Some people open up their hearts, while others set a guard.

Our heart is also like a lamp, it's better when it's lit.
When we are saved, God's spirit is the oil that burns in it.   (Acts 15:8; Rom. 5:5)
We keep it lit and burning bright, awaiting Christ's return.
For those who do not have the oil, their pleading he will spurn.   (Matt. 25:1–13)

They cannot come into his house, his Spirit must reside.
So many do not know God's plan, his church is like a bride.   (2 Cor. 11:2)
And this is why we tell the world that Jesus is the way.
For only those who know the Lord can enter in and stay.

So how can we help people see that Jesus is the way?   (John 14:5)
By spreading seed so it takes root, so they're not cast away.
We toss the seed and pray for them, we cannot be naïve.
Our adversary will make plans so they do not receive.   (Matt. 13:19)

For Satan does not want the world to know Christ as their Lord.
He's blinded most from God's great gift, so often it's ignored.   (Matt. 13:13–15)
But only God can see the heart and know what is inside.   (Ps. 44:21; Acts 15:8)
So we must keep on spreading seeds so people can decide.

The Bible says the heart is like the soil in which we plant.
Not every type lets God's Word sprout, in some it simply can't.
But God can change the soil that's there, so we must throw the seed,
And only God can tend the soil, so their souls can be freed.

This was a parable I read, which seemed quite clear to me,
But as I searched his Word some more, some things I didn't see.
Could it be that a person's soil will change throughout their life?
You never know which seed will land and pierce it like a knife.

A seed you throw might sit on top and never start to sprout.
But maybe God is working there, on cleaning that heart out.   (Acts 16:14)
I always thought that each man's heart described a type of soil,   (Matt. 13:18–23)
I did not think that God, perhaps, could change it with his oil.

How many times has God restored a life that went astray?
We simply need to cast the seed, and then pray for them each day.
Too many times I've messed things up when casting forth God's seed.
I always thought it was my job to make sure they were freed.

I blamed myself when it just sat, like somehow I had failed.
I thought it needed to sprout fast or it had not prevailed.
God's seed can sit and stay alive, the Word is that profound.
God's Spirit works so it can sink and penetrate dry ground.

God is the One who tends the soil, who changes things within.   (Jer. 24:7)
We sow the seed with his good news so they can let him in.
Lord, keep my lamp on fire for you, a heart to save the lost,   (Luke 8:16)
So I am not afraid to share, no matter what the cost.   (2 Tim. 1:7; Rev. 2:10)

The Brother

We all have heard the parable about the prodigal son,
Who squandered his inheritance so he could go have fun.   (Luke 15:13)
I understand the message here: God's grace we haven't earned.
But God said, "Read and focus on," after the son returned.

We know the father ran to him, his heart was filled with glee.   (Luke 15:20)
The other son did not seem pleased but filled with jealousy,   (Luke 15:28)
For he had been the faithful one and stayed to help his dad.   (Luke 15:29)
The prodigal had walked away and made his father sad.

The brother failed to look at how a life had been restored.   (Luke 15:32)
Anger rose inside him for now he felt ignored.
He told himself this wasn't right, that he should be the one
Robed in honor with the ring for all that he had done.   (Luke 15:22)

It made me think about how I react when life can seem unfair,
When good breaks go to people who just slack and do not care.
This is what the brother felt the prodigal had done,
He wasted his inheritance on partying and fun.

How could his dad react this way, to offer him a feast.
He squandered all his dad gave him, his blessings should have ceased.   (Luke 15:30)
I never left, I stayed faithful, I stayed right by his side.   (Luke 15:29)
The son kept digging up these thoughts, his pain would not subside.

How many times have my own thoughts made me feel justified?
How quick I am to disregard the reason my Lord died.
We all are like the prodigal, poor choices we display.
If God were like the brother here, he would have walked away.

The story shows the brother failed to celebrate a life
That came back to his father's house from sinfulness and strife.
One test we face throughout our lives is how we treat our peers.
With happiness when they are blessed, or bitterness and tears?

When they receive the blessings that we thought should come to us,
Often we will hold a grudge and sometimes cause a fuss.
This can make us turn away from happiness and peace.
Search your heart for jealousy, so you can find release.

When someone gets promoted, it should never get us mad.
Anytime a life is blessed should make our hearts feel glad.
Promotion comes from God above, and he's set a path for you.
You must not let resentment build or bitterness accrue.

God can choose who he will bless and when he will withhold.
Don't let envy start to grow; don't give it a foothold.
Thank the Lord for what you have and all he has supplied,
Then you'll avoid the devil's trap; set jealousy aside.

The brother should have felt great joy the younger son returned.   (Luke 15:21)
Just think of all God's lessons that the prodigal had learned.   (Luke 15:28)
But when he heard the father had just killed the fatted calf,
His anger flared at what his dad had done for this riffraff.

Never think that you are better in your Father's eyes.   (Prov. 13:10)
God loves us all since all are flawed, stick close to what is wise.   (Rom. 3:23)
Celebrate the people you work with every day.
This faithfulness God will reward, so blessings come your way.   (Prov. 28:20)

Lessons from Esther

This book of Esther shows that God will take things meant for harm
And use these schemes against our foes, their weapons he'll disarm.   (Ps. 18:47)
He places people in our lives in ways we do not see.
But in a time that he directs, we see how they are key.

Never think that God is shocked by what we see today.
God knows the hearts of evil men, to him they're on display.   (Ps. 44:21)
We also see how God will use our enemies for good.
He controls the universe; things unfold as they should.

Our God gives favor as he wills, like Esther in this book.
Of all the virgins shown to the king, she was the one he took.
Now Mordecai had raised Esther after both her parents died.   (Esther 2:7)
He raised her like she was his own and looked at her with pride.

God knew that there would be a plot to target all the Jews,
But every time a plan was hatched, God made sure they would lose.   (Isa. 54:17)
Haman told the king that Jews would not follow his laws,   (Esther 3:8)
And tricked the king into letting him enforce his evil cause.   (Esther 3:9–11)

What happened next, I must declare, taught me how I should act.
The people prayed and beseeched God, it had a big impact.   (Esther 4:3)
Esther went to meet the king, for which she could be killed.   (Esther 4:11)
When she appeared, he was not mad; in fact, the king was thrilled.   (Esther 5:2)

God used the pride that Haman had to carry out his plan.
The king sought to reward a deed, to celebrate a man.   (Esther 2:21)
Haman's pride made him assume this was his accolade.   (Esther 6:9)
He was shocked when put in charge of Mordecai's parade.   (Esther 6:10)

Since Haman hated Mordecai, this made him quite depressed.   (Esther 6:12)
Instead of Haman gaining fame, his enemy was blessed.
Again, we see how God can use what's meant to knock us down
And turn the bad into a blessing, it ends up as a crown.

We also see God punish those who seek to cause us pain   (Prov. 28:18)
And use the hurt and suffering and turn it for our gain.
Never think that anything can make your future grim,
Our God can conquer anything, so keep your hope in him.   (Ps. 121:7)

We see decrees in Esther's time attacking God's elect,
So don't be shocked in today's world if new laws seem suspect.
The enemy seeks our demise, just like with Mordecai.   (1 Pet. 5:8)
The key is we must be in prayer and trust God will supply.

Do not give up or lose all hope, let hope replace despair.
Realize that God knows all, and go to him in prayer.
This is how we win the war and align with God's Word.
Do not dwell on skirmishes, your focus will get blurred.

Recognize we are at war, but God controls the board.
He moves his pieces back and forth and scatters Satan's horde.
Keep your eyes fixed upon the Lord; he is the King of Kings.
He knows which way each piece must move; he's pulling all the strings.

So let your heart be filled with joy for it will keep you strong.   (Neh. 8:10)
Then pray each day for victory, and praise him with a song.
Our God has seen this all before, his people were oppressed,
So we must stand in unity, trust God, and stay at rest.   (2 Sam. 22:31)

Cast the First Stone

When I was young, I used to think I had life figured out.
I look back at my walk with God, I had no sense of doubt.
But now I know there was a time when I felt full of pride.
I knew the scriptures inside out but never walked in stride.

God made me think just how I was, my Christian state of mind.
Though I had learned, could talk the talk, my speech was not aligned.
For many times when people failed, I sat and judged their deeds.
I cast a stone to knock them down instead of casting seeds.

I liked to think—with arrogance—that I was pleasing God.
And if he saw how I acted, I would receive a nod.
But that's not true; I failed to learn why Jesus said this line,
"He without sin, cast the first stone," the statement seemed benign.   (John 8:7)

The Pharisees knew well the law, but their own hearts were dead.
They didn't care about the girl, only what Jesus said.   (John 8:6)
They liked to flaunt their holiness and loudly boast to all,   (Matt. 23:23–29)
They hoped to use what Jesus said to pin him to a wall.   (Matt. 22:15)

But everyone had recognized how sinful they were too.   (John 8:9)
So they all left, from old to young, their pride had been run through.
Yet why did I not understand what Jesus tried to say,
That all have sinned and fallen short, from God we fell away?

Is it your goal to change their life, or will your pride just swell?
We must think twice before we speak and judge our hearts as well.
For Jesus sees what's in our hearts, our motives he can judge.   (Ps. 44:21)
So now when I start to react, I get a gentle nudge.   (Acts 25:8)

For even Christ came not to judge but to redeem mankind.   (John 12:47)
The Bible states we can't be fair when we are blind.   (Matt. 7:3, 4)
It's not our job to cast the stones but to heal the sick and hurt.   (Luke 9:2)
Attacking them just makes it worse, it makes God's seed inert.

We cannot hope to change the world or even one lost soul,
If we do not reach out in love, for this should be our goal.   (1 Thess. 1:3)
The Bible says we're like a gong, a loud and blaring sound.   (1 Cor. 13:1)
So now, will you cast the first stones or leave them on the ground?

Spirit of Gentleness

As Christians, we are often told how our lives should bear fruit.
Our hearts can be drawn quickly to some, while others don't take root.
One fruit that took some time to grow is that of gentleness.
When I am wronged, I should forgive, not cling to bitterness.

I truly did not understand the traits of gentleness.   (1 Pet. 3:4)
I often thought when used by me, I somehow showed weakness.
But now I see that gentleness requires great strength of will.
It often uses self-control, which is a spiritual skill.

Jesus used this gentleness while others sought to judge.   (Matt. 11:29)
God's gentleness displays mercy, while justice holds a grudge.
This fruit allowed our Lord to make a change in someone's heart.
It showed why he came to forgive, that trait set him apart.

God's purpose is to change a life, not leave it filled with shame. (Gal. 6:1)
Restoring lives and saving the lost is why our Savior came.
His gentleness can open doors that judging closes tight.   (1 Pet. 3:15)
It also softens hardened hearts, so they seek to do right.

This fruit is often hard to bear if hurt by a close friend,
Which often leaves an open wound that most find hard to mend.
But this is where forgiveness sits, combined with gentleness,
To be an ointment for the wound and bitterness suppress.   (Prov. 15:1)

This fruit can be the catalyst to let the healing start.
When things go wrong, it is the way to reach a hardened heart. (Prov. 25:15)
Your gentleness can subdue pain and let hope in the door,
It covers guilt and shame it finds; it lets God's love restore.   (Eph. 4:2)

We go through times when beaten up, when life's taken its toll. (Hosea 11:4)
This is when we need gentleness to help restore our soul.
God's gentleness can build you up and help you rise above.   (2 Sam. 22:36)
It also helps you stay at rest and shows the world your love.   (Phil. 4:5)

As servants of the Lord, we're told to be gentle, not to fight   (1 Tim. 3:3)

For gentleness is God's wisdom, a fruit to set things right.   (James 3:17)

For in God's sight it's beautiful, a person with this gift   (1 Pet. 3:4)

That lets us heal a painful hurt and start to mend a rift.

Great Flaws

The more I pray and talk with God and listen for his voice,
The more I start to scrutinize my every single choice.
The more I hear his voice each day, the more he does reveal.   (Dan. 2:47; Phil. 3:15)
And as he shows me all my flaws, the dirtier I feel.

For God can see into my heart, it is an open book.   (1 Sam. 16:7)
He sees those hidden places where I do not want to look.   (Job 10:13; 28:11)
Conviction starts to squeeze my heart and forces me to see   (John 8:9)
All the things I need to change, the things that hinder me.

The righteousness I have today was purchased by his Son.   (Rom. 5:19)
Only God can cleanse my heart, he is the holy one.   (1 John 1:7)
But when his Spirit shines in me, flaws start to disappear.   (2 Cor. 3:18)
He takes away my shame and guilt and conquers all my fear.   (Pss. 34:5; 118:6)

This doesn't mean I never fail, but I know where to go,
For only with his Spirit's help can I withstand our foe.
So many people are depressed when shame and guilt rule them.
They need to know that God loves us, we're precious like a gem.   (Ps. 72:14)

When Satan whispers in my ear how often I will fail,   (2 Cor. 2:11)
The Holy Spirit lets me know with him, I will prevail.
When Satan brings up past mistakes to fill my heart with shame,
The Spirit shows me Jesus's blood and all that I can claim.

The fact that we all will fall short is no surprise to God.   (Rom. 3:23)
Jesus came to die for us because he knows we're flawed.
Our sin declares we all should die, the debt that all men pay,   (Rom. 6:23)
But when we know him as our Lord, he takes that sting away.   (John 3:15, 16)

So don't let Satan keep you trapped in worry and despair.
Cast it all at Jesus's feet, and your life he will repair.   (Ps. 55:22)
Yes, I am flawed—broken too—but I refuse to quit.
I will not let my life pass by, so I refuse to sit.

Stand up, shout loud for all to hear; no matter what life brings,
With Jesus Christ to strengthen us, the saints can do all things.   (Phil. 4:13)
Let Satan's lies that you're no good or you're too weak to win
Be echoes in the past for you when you let Jesus in.

But this means we must follow him, it means that he must rule.
And let his Spirit work in us so Satan's lies don't fool.   (John 8:44)
It also means we must move on and stop digging up the past.   (Isa. 43:18)
It doesn't matter who we were, with God we are recast.

It's not too late, we're on his wheel, the potter's still at work.   (Isa. 64:8)
His Holy Spirit will reshape; it is a spiritual perk.
We're made anew when on the wheel, long after we are saved.   (2 Cor. 5:17)
The key is letting God shape us, removing sin we craved.

This is where it can be tough once we're in sin's tight grip.
If we do not renew our minds, this can cause us to slip.   (Rom. 12:2)
We battle not against just flesh, we're really in a war.   (Eph. 6:12)
So make sure all your armor's on, or you can get hurt more.   (Eph. 6:11)

Satan knows that you're God's child, he knows the role we play.
He wants you to think you can't win so you don't join the fray.
But greater is our God than him, or any foe we face,   (1 John 4:4)
So even though we have great flaws, God's strength we can embrace.

Death, Where Is Your Sting?

We know that death is part of life, a fact we all must face.
The question is are you prepared when you meet death's embrace?
What happens next is up to you, a choice where you can go,
Eternal life with saints above or torment down below. (John 3:15)

Eternal life is not some myth, it's not some fantasy. (John 10:28)
We simply do not disappear for all eternity.
Since it is real, the question is: at death, where will you go?
The truth is many are deceived, they really do not know. (2 Cor. 4:4)

For heaven's often talked about, where we go when we die.
It's shown as clouds or a sunny sky, with angels flying by.
Some people say that all go there; this is a current trend.
The Bible says that isn't so, some face a different end. (Matt. 7:14)

The Bible says that all have sinned, the reason that we die. (Rom. 6:23)
To God, no one is good enough, no matter how we try. (Rom. 3:23)
So God's own Son has conquered sin and paid the price in full, (Isa. 44:22)
For only Jesus conquered death, escaping from its pull. (Rev. 1:18)

When we accept him as our Lord, our sins are washed away. (Titus 3:5)
The Bible says to get to God, that Christ is the only way. (John 14:6)
He went to Hades when he died and took away the keys.
So death and Hades lost control, their power he did seize. (Rev. 1:18)

Since Jesus now has conquered death, he now controls that door.
So those who are his followers are trapped by sin no more.
The grip of death on all mankind was broken when Christ died, (Acts 2:24)
So we don't worry about death when God is on our side.

Therefore, the Bible states to all, oh death, where is your sting? (1 Cor. 15:55)
The power of our Savior's blood rules over everything. (1 Tim. 6:15)
For Satan's power—yes death itself—lies broken at the cross.
Death and Hades cannot reign since Jesus is their boss.

He is the truth, the way, the life, our sin he did atone,   (John 14:6)
Now who can stand above our Lord who sits upon his throne?   (Ps. 47:8)
So praise the name of Jesus Christ, who claimed the victory,   (1 Cor. 15:57)
Who rose again and is alive for all eternity.   (Rom. 14:9)

Faith Well Versed

The Bible talks about our faith and what it's needed for;   (Hab. 2:4)
Without it, we cannot please God, a fact we can't ignore.   (Heb. 11:6)
The Bible says that it is real, it's more than simply hope,   (Heb. 11:1)
And if we analyze our faith, it has a broader scope.

It activates the spiritual realm, one function of its use.
God's power is seen when faith is used, our words can bind or loose.
It is the anchor for our hope when doubt begins to grow.   (Gal. 5:5)
It's confidence that God's at work before the changes show.   (2 Cor. 5:7)

One trait of faith is that it grows the more that it is used.
And it becomes quite powerful when it and trust are fused.   (Gal 2:20)
But faith can also falter if we let doubt control.
So mixing it with hope and trust should always be our goal.   (1 Pet. 1:21)

We all must speak God's promises, so faith cannot be moved.
No matter what the mountain is, it now can be removed.
The key is keeping our faith pure so hope and faith will rise.   (1 Tim. 3:9)
So we must focus on our God and focus on the prize.   (2 Tim. 4:7)

We must put trust in what God says and not in Satan's lies.   (Rom. 10:17)
We only need a mustard seed; it's not about the size.   (Rom. 12:3)
Our confidence is boosted when we study what God said.   (Eph. 3:12)
We need to know his promises and trust in them instead.   (1 Cor. 2:5)

If we rely on what we know or things that we have heard,   (1 Tim. 1:4)
Then hope will often be attacked, but our faith will not be stirred.
So dwell on things that God proclaims—it is a good report— (Heb. 11:39)
And you will see your faith ignite, so hope will not fall short.

When we are praying for a thing, for God to answer prayer,
Our faith becomes the proof we need, the evidence we wear. (Heb. 10:23)
Since faith will grow when it is used, we must put it in play.
It must be backed up by our words, or our hope soon will stray. (2 Cor. 4:13)

Faith tells us that no matter what, our God has things in hand.
And he will give us stubborn strength, the fortitude to stand.   (2 Thess. 1:4)
God also shares his faith with us when ours is not enough.   (2 Cor. 1:24)
He's closer than a brother is, he stays when times get tough.

Faith is the currency of God, our faith has come from him.   (Phil. 3:9)
It keeps us focused on God's love when our odds can seem slim.   (Gal. 5:6)
It is the catalyst in prayer, so God begins to act.
So even when we see no way, God's plan becomes a fact.

Your faith is seen as righteousness, like Abraham before.   (Rom. 3:28; 4:9)
When things look grim and we grow weak, it opens up the door.
So any mountain can be moved, the promise our faith knows,
For we can do all things in Christ, regardless of our foes.   (Eph. 6:16)

Mental Health

I always thought since I know God, my mind would be a rock.
But then I started getting stressed; it came as quite a shock.
I thought with God that I would coast through any trials that came.
Why did I start to feel this way? It brought on guilt and shame.

My naive view made me believe salvation was enough.
I did not think these challenges would prove to be so tough.   (Acts 20:19)
I realize now I wasn't prepped to face the trials that came.
I thought my knowledge was enough; I was not in the game.

I failed to heed what God's Word said about the trials we face.   (1 Pet. 1:6)
I could have paid an awful price if not for my Lord's grace.   (Eph. 2:5)
Satan wanders like a lion, just looking to destroy.   (1 Pet. 5:8)
He uses guilt and mental stress to take away our joy.

The Bible says the joy of God will be our source of power.
So we must stand on Jesus's name so Satan can't devour.   (1 Pet. 5:8)
The fiercest battle that we face is lies that we accept.   (John 8:44)
But when we wield the sword of truth, we will not fight inept.   (Heb. 4:12)

The helmet of salvation helps to reinforce our mind,
So when we feel the pressure come, God's wisdom we can find.
The Bible says to renew your mind; there is a reason why.   (Rom. 12:2)
It helps defend us when Satan tries to fool us with a lie.

But we must watch what we let in through both our eyes and ears.   (1 Tim. 6:20)
The information we bring in can also strengthen fears.
Anxiety can cripple us, depression can destroy,
But hope can heal a broken heart; God's truth can bring us joy.

As Christians, we must trust in God, our thoughts must dwell on him.
But if we give the world control, our light will start to dim.
The closer you walk to the Lord, the more strength you will gain,
So we must seek to walk with him and in his arms remain.   (Heb. 11:6)

Abide in him and then he abides, he'll give your mind some rest.   (John 15:4)
So when we face the trials life brings, we face them at our best.   (James 1:2)
The Bible does not tell us that with God all problems cease.
But when you walk with him each day, it helps you stay at peace.   (Phil. 4:7)

We know that Satan wants to keep us focused on our pain.
So we give up and do not fight; God's kingdom shows no gain.
We must shake off the doubt he brings and focus on the truth.   (Eph. 6:13)
We know when Satan roars at us, he hasn't got a tooth.

Stay close to God and stay in prayer, hold up his sword and shield.
So when you put his armor on, you never have to yield.   (Eph. 6:11)
Our mental health is up to us, with God we have control.   (Prov. 19:23)
Yet Satan says that we are weak, confusion is his goal.

When we gear up, it shields our mind, our helmet stays secure.
So we stay calm, and ride out the storm, God's strength helps us endure.   (Eph. 6:13; 1 Cor. 10:13)
Then when we feel fatigued and weak, our God defends our soul.   (Ps. 34:7)
His peace and joy we then receive, and they will make us whole.   (Rom. 14:17)

Since the truth that God gives us life never seems too grim,
We will stand fast in anything when our eyes stay on Him.   (2 Cor. 1:21)
So when your mind thinks life's too hard, the struggle is too much,
Remember God is in control, so let your mind feel his touch.   (Ps. 47:8)

What Do You Declare?

The Bible speaks of promises and actions God will take.	(Rom. 9:4)
It also says we must review the choices that we make.	
One choice we make is using words in line with what God says.	
The words you say can hold much weight and declare God's promises.	

How many times have our words failed to help us walk the walk?
This is why we must take care and choose how we will talk.
Our faith declares what we can't see, its words are full of hope.
But doubt declares how bad things are, how tough it is to cope.

Elijah spoke with confidence when God said it would rain.	(1 Kings 18:1)
Declaring this despite a drought, to most would seem insane.	(James 5:17)
He chose those words because we know faith makes him speak aloud	
The promises that God had made before he saw a cloud.	(1 Kings 18:43–44)

Do you stand strong, declaring loud what God puts in your heart?	
Or are your words filled with defeat before the changes start?	(Job 15:5)
How often do your words declare how things are going wrong?	
When they should shout, "God's in control," and praise him in a song.	(Ps. 75:9)

We pray for kids who are off course yet talk of trials they bring.	
We should declare that all our houses will one day serve the King.	(Josh. 24:15)
We speak of debt and all our lack, of what we can't afford.	
We should declare God will provide our blessings he has stored.	

When we are sick, do our words speak of how our body feels?	
Or do we shout about our God, who is the God who heals?	
King David said declare God's works, thank God for what he's done.	(Ps. 9:11; 71:17)
So think about the words you speak, do they promote God's Son?	

The victory is in our words, so do not speak defeat.	
Declare how God can do all things, how God cannot be beat.	(Ps. 71:18)
Our words can loose, or they can bind; it's what the Lord has said.	(Matt. 16:19; 18:18)
Our words speak faith to overcome, or doubt and lack instead.	

It's up to you to choose your words, to change how you will speak.

Your words can focus on what's wrong or breakthroughs that you seek.   (Rom. 3:4)

So speak with faith; release God's power so promises come true.   (1 Kings 3:12; Ps. 18:30)

Remember that God's promises must be declared by you.

His Most Prized Possession

As humans, we are gatherers, we like collecting things.
Antiques, fine clothes, or even shoes, they make us feel like kings.
But often there's a favorite, one thing above the rest.
And though we may like many things, this one we like the best.

A "prized possession" it is called, since it brings us much joy,
For even when we were just kids, we had a favorite toy.
It's human nature to find joy in special things we own,
Mounted and framed, stored on a shelf, or saved into our phone.

Now when we look at God above, who made the universe,
The planets, stars, and galaxies, these things are so diverse.
Though they show off God's handiwork, their value won't increase.
There's only one that God proclaims to be his masterpiece.   (Eph. 2:10)

Of all creation, God tells us, just one he has adored.   (Prov. 8:22)
He even sacrificed his Son so they could be restored.
"For God so loved," the Bible states, a statement that is true.   (John 3:16)
His prized possession has a name: His favorite one is you.

For you are made in God's image, no other can compare.   (1 Cor. 11:7)
And he knew you before your birth, created with much care.   (Jer. 1:5)
So when you feel you are no good or don't deserve God's love,
Remember that he crafted you, handmade by God above.   (Ps. 8:5)

Don't listen to the devil's lies; he knows whose child you are.
He'll tell you that you're too far gone, your value is subpar.
He whispers, "God is mad at you," when you make a mistake.
He's worried that you'll know your rights, his strongholds you will break.

He wants you to feel too depressed so you feel tired and weak.
In Eden, he stole us from God, and our future then looked bleak.
But God would not let us be lost; he came up with a plan.
One that Satan couldn't see: He came to earth as man.   (John 3:13)

There is no other one like you, the apple of God's eye.   (Ps. 17:8)

To win us back from sin and shame, he sent his Son to die.

So never think you're unworthy, a failure, a mistake.

There was no price God wouldn't pay when your soul was at stake.   (Isa. 44:22)

Strangely Dim

There is a song I love to sing that makes my stress decrease.
The song tells us to turn our eyes; it makes my soul at peace.   (Psa. 119:37; Isa. 17:7)
To make our Lord our focal point, to fix our eyes on him,
Then all the troubles our world brings will soon grow strangely dim.

For if we keep our gaze on Christ, we never will lose hope.
For then when troubles come our way, we will have the strength to cope.
When we fix our eyes on him, his power we will see,
We understand just who Christ is, the God of eternity.   (Isa. 43:13)

So now we see the big picture, where God controls it all.   (Dan. 2:21)
He guides our steps, makes straight our paths, he has the final call.
Yet often we still live with fear and let depression win.   (Isa. 41:10; Luke 12:32)
Emotions start to take control, which brings more trouble in.   (Luke 21:34)

How we live life is up to us, it's where we fix our gaze.
If it's on Christ, there's victory, if not the trouble stays.
For Jesus is the truth, the way, he also is the life.   (John 14:6)
When we seek out his will each day, we dodge much pain and strife.

When Christ is centered in your life, some troubles still find you.
The difference is now you see them from God's point of view.
There is no mountain too high, no problem that's too large,
For who can stand against our God, he is the one in charge.

The key is will you look to him? Will you lift your eyes?
No problem you will ever face can catch God by surprise.
If we follow what God says, the best path will be shown.
A mountain only seems too high when we face it alone.

This is a choice we all must make, to turn our eyes or not.
So we must choose this every day; this battle must be fought.
For when we look upon his face, our troubles melt away.
Worship him who rules it all, and gain strength when you pray.

Rejoice in what our Lord has done and all that he will do.
For greater is our God with us, our strength he will renew.
We must turn our eyes to God and keep our thoughts on him.
For only then will mountains shrink and worry start to dim.

Stand Fast

It's funny how when trouble comes our mind begins to spin.
How thoughts begin to permeate of why we'll never win.
Our mind feels like it's under siege, it makes our chest squeeze tight.
It makes us draw back from the world, we're in a spiritual fight.

Our world can start to overload, and we let down our guard.   (Ps. 141:3)
So focusing on what God says now suddenly is hard.
Since everything that's happening keeps racing through our mind,
The peace of God that comforts us is difficult to find.   (Col. 3:15; Phil. 4:7)

We start to dwell on obstacles and mountains that we face.
We fail to see the promises that God has put in place.   (Heb. 6:12)
But we have got the greatest friend, who knows what will unfold,
With him beside us, we can rise and make a stand that's bold.

For God sees all—from start to end—and cannot be outplayed.   (Job 34:21)
When God's with us, whatever comes, we need not be afraid.   (Deut. 31:8)
He guards our path and makes it straight when we don't see a way.   (Prov. 21:8; 4:11)
No matter what life throws at us, God guides us every day.   (Ps. 48:14)

When Satan tries to bring us down, God makes it our strength.
For every time we get attacked, God's shield will add more length.
For who can stand against our God when he has formed a plan?   (Isa. 14:27)
Even if doubt should start to grow, we serve a God who can.

Though Satan plots to vanquish us, our God can raise us up.   (1 Pet. 5:9)
He gives us strength when we are weak if we drink from his cup.   (Joel 3:10)
For sickness cannot overcome the saints who stand as one.   (Matt. 18:20; 1 Thess. 5:11)
We only need to read God's Word and look at what he's done.   (Ps. 66:16)

Our fervent prayers can conquer much when sickness knocks us down.   (James 5:16)
We serve a God who wants to heal, the King who wears the crown.   (Exod. 15:26; Ps. 103:3)
Jehovah Rapha is his name, the God who wants to heal.
Stand on the promises he gives, not on just how you feel.

Another thing that we must do, we must choose to stand.   (1 Cor. 16:13)
Satan hopes we will give up, we won't see what God planned.
For victory is ours to claim; we have already won.
We simply must declare his Word and join our hands as one.   (Eccles. 4:12)

The key is doing what God asks and trusting in his Word.   (2 Pet. 1:5)
Take the time to study it so your faith can be stirred.   (2 Tim. 2:15)
The scriptures tell us many times what God has promised us.
Yet we must stand upon these things, which others find absurd.   (Luke 9:2)

For faith is how we activate the promises God gave.   (Ps. 116:6)
This means that we must trust in them when thoughts tell us to cave.
We must hold fast in hope and faith that God can make us whole.   (Rom. 15:4)
No matter what life throws at us, our God is in control.   (Ps. 47:8)

The Father of Lies

When man was made by God himself, a special bond was born.	(Gen. 9:6)
But when man ate the forbidden fruit, our special bond was torn.	(Gen. 3:6)
Mankind was fooled by Satan's lie, that we can be like God,	(Gen 3:5)
One little bite was all it took; from then, mankind was flawed.	

Man used to walk with God each day, but now he hides afraid.	(Gen. 3:8)
Our bond was torn when fear appeared, a hefty price was paid.	(Gen. 3:23)
"Father of lies," our foe is called; he whispers in our ear.	(Phil. 4:7)
Where God brings peace and unity, Satan brings strife and fear.	(Col. 3:15)

He lies today; he's still the same as many go astray.	
The Bible says he blinds the lost, his lies turn man away.	(2 Cor. 4:4)
So we must know what God's Word says so we don't get deceived.	(Deut. 11:16)
Then we must spread the Word of God to combat lies believed.	

The Bible says that even we, as Christians, can be fooled.	(Luke 21:8)
So take the time to learn God's Word and its teachings, be well schooled.	
For then we can renew our minds and strengthen how we walk.	(Rom. 12:2)
Our enemy will accuse us; God's teachings he will mock.	

Subtle lies and partial truths are weapons he will use.	(Gen. 3:1)
He hopes that we will doubt our God, his plan is to confuse.	
He'll tell us why we're powerless; he wants to bring us shame	
When actually, he knows we hold the power of Christ's name.	(1 Cor. 5:4)

He wants to take the peace and joy that God wants for our lives,	(Gal. 5:22; Rom. 15:3)
And rip apart the bond God made for husbands and their wives.	
He whispers how our spouses fail, of all they need to do.	(Ps. 36:1)
He promotes strife and arguments; resentments he will brew.	(Prov. 16:28)

The Bible says he's like a lion seeking to destroy.	(1 Pet. 5:8)
Deception is his tool of choice to take away our joy.	(Heb. 3:3)
Our families are gifts from God, they're meant to bless our life.	
But Satan wants to ruin that with lies and tears and strife.	

But God knows what is best for us, his plan is always right.   (1 Sam. 2:3)
We need him as our focus to rely on his insight.
In everything we choose to do, we need his help to guide.
Our life is better every day with Jesus at our side.

For happiness is knowing that our God will never leave.   (Heb. 13:5)
No matter what we face each day, his strength we will receive.
For greater is my Lord, my King, than battles I will face,
Knowing that I feel his peace when I'm in his embrace.

So when I hear the devil's lies, the ones he hopes I choose,
If I can stay aligned with God, my enemy will lose.
The joy and peace I feel today come from my God above.   (Neh. 8:10; Ps. 28:7)
The strife and pain I used to feel are now replaced with love.

The Army of the Lord

Sometimes I feel I'm under siege, shots fired everywhere.
Battles seem to rush at me; sometimes it's hard to bear.
The good news is I'm not alone, it's not a solo fight.
When I feel like I am pinned down, his strength increases might.

As Christians, we are in a war, the battleground foretold.
We either choose to sit and watch or gear up and be bold.
The Bible says that we should rise and fight for God each day,　　　(Ezek. 37:10)
But sometimes I get overwhelmed when I don't stop and pray.

A soldier does not go to war without his sword and shield.
You need to put your armor on or battles you may yield.
We must prepare for war each day, God's armor girded tight.
Only then can we prevail when we are called to fight.

The time grows short to save the lost, we're in the war today.
All of us are needed now, we have a part to play.
Some troops can fight on the front line, the infantry of God.
They run into the combat zone, a feat I do applaud.

Some are like the cavalry, they charge on God's command.
They trample on the devil's troops with God's Word in their hand.
They come to help the infantry when battles become fierce.
They turn the tide on Satan's horde, his strongholds they will pierce.

My favorite group that God will use does damage we don't see.
They pick apart the enemy like snipers from a tree.
They're called by God to pray nonstop, they have a strong attack.
These warriors are snipers who push Satan's forces back.

However, we must not neglect the medics of our King.
The Christians who step in to help, their praises we must sing.
They clothe and feed the hurting troops and care for family.
Without these troops, some would withdraw or face anxiety.

The army of the Lord, of course, has Jesus in the lead.   (Joel 2:11)
He directs the battle plans his father has decreed.
For who can stand against our God? His plans are never wrong.
Every foe will one day bow, no enemy's too strong.

With God in charge we'll always win, each battle is the Lord's.
Let God command where you will go to conquer Satan's hordes.
God drafted us to be with him, he conquered sin and death,
So I will serve and fight with him with my remaining breath.

Whatever role he puts you in, remember you will need
To spend some time in prayer each day, so his voice you can heed.
Wear shoes of peace, so you will know just where and when to fight.
Ensure you have his helmet on and buckle it real tight.

When Satan tries to come at you, the sword you'll quickly wield.
And when the enemy attacks, make sure you have your shield.
The shield of faith will help you stand when battles seem so long.
His belt of truth you can secure to help your faith stay strong.

So you can fight in victory, no matter what your role,
And God will keep you safe from harm, the keeper of your soul.
Since time is short 'til he comes back, we must seek out the lost.
We need to set the captives free, no matter what the cost.

Exposed Yet Covered

The Word of God exposes sin, it looks inside my heart.   (Heb. 4:12)
It points out how I've come up short; it's like a doctor's chart.
The Holy Spirit will convict, so he can help me change.   (John 16:8)
Correction with a touch of love, a concept I find strange.   (Prov. 3:11; 10:17)

Now Satan, on the other hand, will try to pile on guilt.
He hopes to fill me full of shame, so my strength starts to wilt.   (Prov. 11:2; 13:18)
He uses every time I've failed as proof to build his case
That I do not deserve God's love, I don't deserve God's grace.

He wants my sin to stay exposed, accusing me each day.   (Rev. 12:10)
So as a Christian, I give up, on the sidelines I will stay.
For he knows who I am in Christ, he knows what I can do.   (Phil. 4:13)
So he will try to keep me bound with condemnation too.   (Rom. 8:1)

But Jesus sets the captives free, so I will not give up.   (Isa. 42:7; Luke 4:18)
He died so I could conquer sin, his Spirit lifts me up.   (1 Cor. 15:57)
Forgiveness, grace, and mercy too are gifts he gives to me.
I only need to come to him, repent, and be set free.   (Rev. 3:3)

The Bible says God never leaves, he stays to calm my fears.
When Satan tries to bring me down, my Savior dries my tears.   (Rom. 10:11)
The blood of Jesus cleanses sin, forgiveness is the cure.
If I repent and turn to him, his blood will make me pure.

God's mercy will endure each day, his grace he will provide.
He knows the battles I will face; it was for me that he died.
So how can I repay the cost of what God did for me?
I know the price that my sin cost, the cost to set me free.   (Rom. 6:23)

So God must then expose those things he knows will hold me back.   (Heb. 4:13)
Only when they are removed can I get back on track.
Sometimes it's hard to deal with things; the scars that bring much pain.
But every time I deal with these, it helps remove a chain.   (Ps. 116:16)

He wants to root out all my sin; it's not to punish me.
He wants me full of joy and strength, the best that I can be.   (Rev. 16:15)
Those buried things he will reveal, he washes off the mud.   (2 Cor. 4:2)
So even when I feel exposed, I'm covered by his blood.   (Ps. 85:2)

Who Answers Your Door?

As Christians, we must think about the choices that we make,
How often we don't realize that blessings are at stake.
When trouble comes, do we respond with faith or simply fear?   (Mark 4:40)
One stops the trouble in its tracks, the other draws it near.

If we let fear control our minds, we can't trust in the Lord.
We override what God has said, a choice we can't afford.
We know we must renew our minds, but here's the reason why: (Rom. 12:2)
The enemy tries to deceive us, so we believe a lie.

Fear whispers that we will stay sick when faith says our God heals.
Fear points to all our aches and pains and how our body feels.
Faith tells us God is in control and has the final say,
That we should ask our God to heal as part of how we pray.

Fear brings worry to our life and shows what we can lose.
Faith lets us see the bigger scene; eternity we choose!   (Rom. 3:28)
We must choose how to live each day, to trust in God, or not.   (Ps. 20:7)
So why not take what God provides, what Jesus's blood has bought?

Or you can let fear dictate things, be worried constantly,
So Satan then directs your life when Jesus set you free.
Your victory starts in your mind as trouble starts to knock.   (Ps. 91:5–7)
Do you let fear and doubt walk in, or do you have a lock?   (2 Cor. 5:7)

I know that we must all face trials, with battles that are rough.
Everyone will face big things; these giants can be tough.
But do you act as David did, run charging at your foe?   (1 Sam. 17:48)
Or when the obstacle seems great, does your strength start to go?

Remember who is at our side, who always has our back.   (Ps. 118:6)
His Word is full of strategy when we're under attack.   (Prov. 3:5)
The joy God brings becomes our strength, his faith replaces fear.   (Isa. 41:10)
His peace makes worry obsolete, so trust can now stand clear.   (Ps. 29:11)

So, think about how you respond, does trouble make you stressed?
Or have you put your trust in God, so you can find his rest?   (Isa. 30:15)
For either faith or fear will come, the choice is up to you.
God tells us how to strengthen faith, and our minds we must renew.

You need to have God's Word inside, so you can conquer fear.   (Rom. 10:17)
Your walk with God must remain close, and then his voice you can hear.
When trouble knocks upon your door, let your faith answer it,
So you can keep your peace and joy, so you stay mentally fit.

We can't control what life deals out; we choose how we'll react.
Our God gives us the strength to fight, our armor stays intact.   (Rom. 4:20)
Put God in first place and trust in him; remember who you face.   (Eph. 6:16)
And even when you feel worn out, God helps us run our race.

Silver and Gold

The Bible speaks of craving things; it also speaks of greed.
Our world will try to dictate all the things that we will need.
We're inundated every day by media and ads.
Our phones will even tell us why we need the latest fads.

The danger is we get caught up in what the world desires.
We strive to get more earthly things, an urge that never tires.
Remember that our foe wants us to follow him instead.   (Prov. 11:28)
That is why he works so hard to get inside our head.

He wants our focus fixed on him and not upon our Lord.
So he shows us these fancy toys we know we can't afford.
Success, we're told, is based on all these things we can acquire,
Even though eternally, these things will all expire.   (Prov. 27:24)

That is why the Bible says that we must stay on guard.   (Mark 10:25)
This world will try to mislead us, and ignoring this is hard.
What profit does it bring to us if greed costs us our soul?   (Mark 8:36)
Eternal life is what we seek, it must remain our goal.

Prosperity can be a trap if it becomes our god.   (Matt. 19:23, 24)
It promises to keep us safe; this notion is quite flawed.
We must remember everything first comes from God above.   (Hag. 2:8)
We cannot let these earthly wants become our one true love.

Yet this does not mean I believe prosperity is bad.
The Bible shows us many times the blessings people had.
God wants us to have joy and peace, and to trust he will provide.   (Luke 6:38)
Jehovah Jireh is his name, and our needs he has supplied.

Yet sometimes we do not perceive why God has closed a door.   (Hosea 14:9; Job 11:7)
Sometimes he still is teaching us some things we can't ignore.
It matters not how much we have, but what we use it for.
Is giving what we want to do or is it just a chore?

Jehovah Jireh never fails; he is our best resource.
Silver and gold all come from him; he is the one true source.   (Hag. 2:8)
If we seek God with all our hearts, his riches we will find.   (Matt. 6:33)
Not all his blessings are of gold, some are another kind.

When Peter said he had no gold or silver to donate,   (Acts 3:6)
The crippled man was not impressed since begging was his fate.
What Peter gave was greater still, more than he could have dreamed.
His legs were healed, his faith restored, his life had been redeemed.

The power that is in Christ's name can always do much more,   (1 Cor. 5:4; Phil. 2:10)
No matter how much gold you have or wealth that you could store.
Though gold can help a man in need, it cannot pay our debt.
For we know Jesus died for us, so eternal life we get.   (John 20:31)

My Redeemer Lives

Everyone will face hard times with struggles that ensue.
And whether you have faith or not, these things will come at you.
For even Job—who walked with God, with whom God was well pleased—　　(Job 1:8)
Had to face some horrific things which were not quickly eased.

His servants and his oxen killed, his sheep consumed by fire,　　(Job 1:14–16)
His camels gone, his children dead, his problems seemed quite dire.　　(Job 1:17–19)
Satan attacked his body, too, just as he had his wealth.
Not only did Job lose a lot, he also lost his health.　　(Job 2:7)

How often do we cry to God when facing just one thing?
Just like Job, we will face trials that often hurt or sting.
How many times do we lose faith when things don't go our way?
How many times do we lose hope and beg God when we pray?

You think that with what Job went through, his hope would soon recede,
That Job would curse his God above, and Satan would succeed.
For how much pain can one man take when everything seems lost?
But Job knew who his anchor was, his faith could not be tossed.

Job ripped his clothes and shaved his head and then fell on the ground.　　(Job 1:20)
He worshipped God, how could this be when chaos did abound?
Job's grief was great, he was a man whose children all were slain.　　(Job 1:19)
His friends showed up to comfort him and found a man in pain.　　(Job 2:13)

His wife told him to just curse God and then he should just die.　　(Job 2:9)
How many times when we're in pain does Satan tell this lie?
Satan declares you'll never win, so you should just give up.
That God will never rescue you as too often you've messed up.　　(Isa. 44:22)

The lesson here is not about how things in life go wrong.
The lesson here is our God lives, so our faith should be strong.
While Job sat and mourned his loss, he finally realized
That his God reigned in all affairs, and this world he supervised.　　(Job 5:8–14)

Job recognized the power of God, who pulled on all the strings.   (1 Cor, 2:5)
He bound and loosed as he saw fit, from paupers up to kings.   (Job 12:18, 19)
The wicked can't gain victory; their triumph will be short.   (Job 20:5)
For God will always vindicate, their evil plans he'll thwart.

Job pondered what his life had meant, the reason he was there.
Futility had crossed his mind and almost brought despair.   (Job 7)
The key is not what Job went through, as bad as that would be,
The key is how he handled it; his faith is what we see.

Yet as Job talked among his friends, he started to get vexed,   (Job 19:2)
So heed what Job responded with, the words that came out next:
I know that my redeemer lives, and this I shall decree,   (Job 19:25)
My lips shall not speak wickedly while breath is part of me.   (Job 27:3, 4)

Our friends will often try to help in battles we go through.
But only God can strengthen faith, a gift he gives to you.   (Rom. 10:17; Eph. 2:8)
The key is knowing whose we are, that we are his redeemed.   (Gal. 3:3; 1 Pet. 1:18–19)
You cannot be defeated when with God you have been teamed.

So rejoice in this awesome fact that your redeemer lives.
Then speak aloud for all to hear for victory he gives.   (Ps. 107:2)
So no matter what you face each day, just praise the risen Lord,   (Luke 24:34)
For when the trials of life approach, in God your hope is stored.   (Ps. 31:24; Lam. 3:24)

Communion Revisited

As Christians, we have been involved or witnessed in our church
Where everyone has bread or wine, so I did some research.
I read about how Christ broke bread and what he had to say.
I also looked at what Paul wrote when things had gone astray.

I next looked at what the Word said communion meant.
The meaning of the word itself did also help augment.
Communion is the sharing of a feeling or a thought,
An intimate expression that most often means a lot.

Yet growing up I used to think communion was a sign,
A tradition that the churches did that often came with wine.
I thought it simply symbolized what Christ had done for me.
I never thought I needed to be ready spiritually.

When eating bread as you partake, do you look deep inside?
It represents all that Christ did and how on that cross he died.
His body paid the price for us, so our souls could be saved.
So we must also die to self; we cannot be enslaved.

His blood, the wine, means so much more, we should proceed with awe.
The power that his blood displays removes us from the law.   (Rom. 6:14)
It was his blood that cleansed our sin, the sacrificial lamb,   (John 1:29)
It represents our covenant, like God's with Abraham.

We must approach this sacrament, recalling what he gave.
His blood was spilt to save us all, redeeming us from the grave.   (Ps. 49:15)
We need to drink in humbleness, with thanks upon our tongue,
For Jesus conquered sin and death when on that cross he hung.

Paul warned the church to not take lightly this sacred thing we do,   (1 Cor. 11:27)
You need to honor God in this, or it will impact you.
You must look hard at how you live. Is God first every day?   (1 Cor. 11:28)
How often are you praising him? How often do you pray?

Apostle Paul had told the church how they had veered off course.
Communion was a spectacle, not focused on its source.   (1 Cor. 11:20–22)
They had forgotten the biggest part, remembering our Lord.
Their focus should have been on him, that part they had ignored.

So take the time to look inside and judge what God can see.   (1 Cor. 11:31)
The Bible says we curse ourselves if we are not worthy.   (1 Cor. 11:29)
So take the time to seek the Lord, confessing all your sin,
For only when we seek his face can work be done within.

It's better that God chastens us so condemnation's done.   (Rom. 8:1)
And when we let the Spirit lead, we focus on God's Son.
Communion is a special thing where we remember Christ.
We thank him for all he has done and what he sacrificed.   (Ps. 100:4)

It also is where we look deep at how we live our lives.
And we need to remember this before the bread arrives.
We need to seek what God would say about the life we lead.
Then listen to what he tells us and what his Word decreed.

God knows that we will go off course and that we will still fall short.
That's why we must confess our sins so we get God's support.   (1 John 1:9)
We know that God forgives our sins when we ask fervently.
So when communion is observed, take it joyfully.

El Shaddai
(Our God Is All-Sufficient)

We know our God has many names describing who he is.
They also are a promise to the chosen he calls his.
Jehovah Jireh will provide, stored blessings he reveals.   (Phil. 4:19)
Jehovah Rapha keeps us strong; he is the God who heals.

With all the struggles we face now, at times we find it rough.
Remember God is El Shaddai, he always is enough.   (Gen. 35:11)
Sometimes our problems seem too big to ever go away.
We can't forget our loving God, who has the final say.

We serve a God who sees it all, beginning and the end,   (Ps. 90:2)
Who stays with us and loves us, so there is no better friend.   (Heb. 13:5; Prov. 18:24)
This title says he does much more than simply meet our needs.
So many times when God helps us, our wishes he exceeds.

We serve a God who goes before, who keeps our footing sure,   (Deut. 1:30; Ps. 119:105)
Who meets our needs despite our foe, who uses schemes to lure.
El Shaddai means more than enough; it's why he's called I Am.   (Exod. 3:14)
There is no problem he can't solve as Saviour, King, and Lamb.

As El Shaddai, he can repair all aspects of our lives.
This allows our faith to stand 'til victory arrives.   (Prov. 21:31)
And knowing God can meet each need, will light his oil within,
So we stand strong as hope bursts forth that we can conquer sin.

The thought that first comes to my mind when I hear "El Shaddai,"
It's how his faithfulness abounds, and on him I can rely.   (Deut. 32:4)
I find it hard to comprehend how he rules everything.
No matter what I'm dealing with, I know my friend is King.

The key to serving El Shaddai is giving him control.
A task I often struggle with, it needs to be my goal.
For only when I trust in him can God surpass my plans.
His Word tells me I must submit and leave things in his hands.   (Job 22:21)

Now every time I'm overwhelmed and feel myself get stressed,
I know I serve almighty God, and I can find his rest.   (Gen. 17:1)
Thus I can stand like saints of old with God who is enough.
No enemy can stand against, no problem is too tough.   (Prov. 21:30)

The Sacrifice of Praise

When I first think of sacrifice, I do not think of praise.
I did not truly understand the meaning of this phrase.
I always thought we praised our God when things had gone our way.
I did not think it was part of life and needed every day.

I thought we made a sacrifice when we did something wrong.
I always thought that blood was shed, not praising with a song.
With sacrifice, there's something lost, a cost to you and me.
The ultimate was when Christ died and hung upon a tree.

So how is praise a sacrifice as it seems quite opposite?
It is because it's hard to do when we're tossed in the pit.
It's easy to give praise to God when good things start to bloom.
It's harder when we have a child still on the path of doom.

It's hard to praise when doctors say we will get worse each day.
Or creditors are at your door, demanding that you pay.
A sacrifice of praise involves a choice to trust the Lord.
It's lining up with what God says, so we are in accord.

So Job did this when everything was taken from his life,   (Job 19:25)
When he was told to kill himself, advice from his wife.
When everything is stripped from you, could you still look to God?
It's not an easy answer since our faith is often flawed.

Take Jonah who had heard from God; it was an epic tale.
He tried to run the other way but got eaten by a whale.   (Jon. 1:17)
When all seemed lost and hope was gone, when nothing went as planned,
He offered up a sacrifice that got him to dry land.   (Jon. 2:10)

His sacrifice of praise to God, "Let God be merciful,"   (Jer. 33:11)
Even though his actions proved to be quite disgraceful.
There's power when we praise our Lord despite the way we feel.
Praising him when we are weak can cause our God to heal.

Praising him when money's tight can help unlock a door.
Blessings start to flow to us like none we've seen before.
So that is why God indicates to do this all the time.   (Heb. 13:15)
This sacrifice is powerful, and from our pit we climb.

God honors those most diligent to thank him in all things.
And praising God rejuvenates, like water from wellsprings.
God controls the universe, so praise him every day,
Even when we're overwhelmed, and things don't go our way.

WEEK 98

Immobilized by Fear

What happens when you face a threat that leaves you paralyzed?
When your world starts to fall apart, your faith feels neutralized.
When panic starts to rise in you, you're dizzy and quite flushed.
When suddenly it's hard to breathe, your chest feels like it's crushed.

Sometimes when arrows fly at us, the enemy comes quick,
Hoping fear can cripple us, so we feel weak and sick.
As Christians, often we believe we're ready to pull back.
But what if fear will not subside while under great attack?

Our mind spins, immobilized, so we don't start to pray.
Then Satan causes fear and doubt to lodge in us and stay.
When every thought says it's too much, our path seems hard to bear.
That is when we must dig deep and look to God for air.　　　　(Rom. 8:15)

The adversary comes at us to stop what God has planned.
He knows that when we trust in God, we always can withstand.　　(Gen. 15:1)
He also knows where we are weak and where he can gain ground.　(Job 3:25)
Therefore, we must seek out God's truth; in his Word strength is found.

When the battle is intense, a victory's close at hand,
Satan uses everything he has at his command.　　　　　　　　　(1 Pet. 5:8)
He tells us why we should be mad, how life is so unfair.
He causes us to spiral down so we don't turn to prayer.　　　　(Judg. 1:20)

He tells us all that will go wrong, how bad our life will get.　　(John 8:44)
How we should quit and run away, how our job is a threat.
We start to feel we cannot cope and that we should call it quits.
We start to doubt what God has said as we endure this blitz.

We fail to call on God for help and do not stand on his Word.　　(Ps. 118:5)
We often whine about our pain; our focus then gets blurred.
We ask our God to save the day when God says rise and fight.　　(Isa. 50:8)
We think that we are powerless when his name gave us might.　　(Deut. 31:8)

It feels like we are taken back to where we had escaped.
Like somehow God had not saved us; in darkness, we are draped.
Where fear and pain consume our life, where God seems far away,   (James 4:8)
Where pressure seeks to knock us down, so powerless each day.

But these are lies that once held us since God has set us free.   (Isa. 43:5)
And when God says that we are free, believing it is key.   (Rev. 1:17)
So turn to praise and thanksgiving instead of fear and doubt.
Study what God promised us, then climb up high and shout.

I will trust God with all my heart, with everything in me.   (Prov. 3:5)
I will not trust what I have heard; from those lies, I will flee.
I'll look to God in all I do, and he will guide my way.   (Prov. 3:6)
And God will keep me safe and whole; he walks with me each day.   (Prov. 3:8)

Blurred Vision

How do we find God's clarity when we look at our life?
How can we walk in peace and joy when our world lives in strife?   (Rom. 14:17)
How can we learn to fix our gaze on God and him alone?
These are skills God's Spirit gives, talents we must hone.

Why is it hard to hear God's voice, decisions hard to make?
When faced with challenges so tough, my future seems at stake.
It is because we're in a fight with what we think we know.   (Rom. 7:23)
Our minds will try to intervene where God wants us to go.

The Bible says to look to God, not simply trust our mind,   (Prov. 3:5)
For often when we trust in this, we end up in a bind.
It does not mean to ignore truth or act without our brains,
But simply giving God control by handing him the reins.   (Ps. 118:8)

The devil tries to hinder us with fear and doubt as well.   (Prov. 29:25)
He whispers the problems we will face, the lies he tries to sell.   (Ps. 37:7)
That is why the Bible says we must control our mind,
For if we do not rule our thoughts, we stumble forward blind.   (Prov. 4:19)

It's hard to see which way to go, our vision can be blurred.
When contradicting voices play, whose message have we heard?
For Satan tries to misdirect and counter God's advice,   (Gal. 5:10)
To keep us guessing what to do, so we just roll the dice.

So we must take the time to stop, to be still like God asks.   (Ps. 46:10)
For if we live a frantic pace, we get caught up in tasks.
Only when we tune God in can we tune our world out.   (Ps. 73:28)
Taking time with God each day will help disperse our doubt.

This battle that we face each day can sometimes feel intense.
So this is where God's Word comes in, it is our best defense.
Just think of when the Lord himself was tempted by our foe.
The enemy knew God's Word, too, and used it as ammo.   (Matt. 4:1–11)

So make sure you know God's Word well; your sword has a sharp blade.   (Heb. 4:12)
Then when you hear the devil's lies, it will come to your aid.
We wrestle not with flesh and blood, the true foe isn't there.   (Eph. 6:12)
We fight against the evil one, and power's in the air.

But we know that far greater still is God who dwells within.   (1 John 4:4)
For only when we trust in God can we be sure to win.
If what you think brings fear and stress, it did not come from God.   (2 Tim. 1:7)
It comes from he who wants that role but we know is a fraud.

For joy and peace are gifts from God; they are our strength also.   (Neh. 8:10)
But any thought that cripples you comes from the pit below.
God's way is best, his burden light, he is our best resource.   (Matt. 11:30)
And if we keep our eyes on him, he'll help direct our course.   (Ps. 119:105)

Truth or Dare

As kids we used to play a game, the one called truth or dare.
You had the choice to tell the truth or risk a task unfair.
I look at all the stunts we did, the bruises I got dealt,
A cut or scrape was easier than telling how we felt.

God showed me how with human hearts, this principle applies.
The truth he gives will set them free, but instead, they trust in lies.   (Ps. 25:10)
They wear a mask so people think their life is in control.
Their actions hide their brokenness, a heart that isn't whole.   (Rom. 11:20)

They'd rather risk eternal life than let God ease their pain.   (Ps. 30:9)
They simply do not understand; for them, our Lord was slain.   (John 3:17)
With Christ you can reveal the truth, he is your closest friend.   (Prov. 18:24)
You do not need to worry if your secrets will offend.

Yet there are times when I still hide, withdraw from God's own Son,
When I feel guilt or foolish pride, ashamed of what I've done.
When I choose dare, a foolish choice, since God knows everything.
When I risk pain and brokenness, when I choose suffering.   (Ps. 32:3)

Realize you have a friend who knows just who you are,
Who knows your pain, your weaknesses, who's witnessed every scar.   (1 John 3:20)
The freedom that this knowledge brings, this gift I can't compare.
Since I can tell him anything, I never need to pick dare.   (Phil. 4:6)

I share my hurts and release my pain, they do not have to stay.
With God it's more like truth and care, he lifts me when I pray.   (Phil. 4:6)
So as I talk and walk with him, I never have to fear.
He brings me joy and happiness; he wipes away each tear.

It's easy now to face my fear; I can confess my sin.   (Prov. 28:13)
With Jesus, I will choose the truth to help me cleanse within.   (1 John 1:9)
I do not need to risk more pain while hiding who I am.
My God loves me, he sent his Son, redeemed by God's own Lamb.   (John 1:29)

So do not choose to play this game; with God, pick truth today.
Take the time to talk to him, and confess your sin each day. (Ps. 32:5)
Then you can ease the pain to come, less scars will be incurred.
With Christ you take the safest route, eternal life ensured. (Rom. 10:9)

🌺 WEEK 101

On a Shelf

I hear God speaking quietly, revealing things to me,   (Ps. 85:8)
Explaining what I need to do with fruit for all to see.
How many times do I neglect to listen when God asks?
How many souls could I have reached if I fulfilled his tasks?

I know I'm on the potter's wheel; God's sculpting is not done.   (Isa. 64:8)
My soul cries out to God above, "I want to serve your Son."
I have an ache to better serve, to follow him each day.
Yet when I look at all I do, my life seems in the way.

So many things that I've put first, that should be cast aside,   (1 Cor. 7:35)
I feel like sand found on a beach, just carried by the tide.
But then I hear within my heart, *Just serve me where you are,*   (John 12:26)
Just put me first at work or home, or even in your car.

It does not matter where I am, no circumstance stops God.   (Job 41:10)
Thinking that my life's too full is reasoning that's flawed.
We do not wait 'til life is slow to make time for the Lord   (Rev. 17:14)
For even when life seems too full, he must not be ignored.

Then God showed me his servant John on Patmos, stuck in jail,
He served the Lord when things looked dire, his body getting frail.
Yet John still carried out God's will while shackled in restraints.
His visions true while put in chains, encouraging the saints.

So who am I to whine to God that I just need more time,
When I should praise the God who reigns in worship, song, and rhyme.   (Ps, 34:1; 45:1)
We often say make time for God, like it's a separate thing.
When God is with us all day long, he's part of everything.   (Matt. 1:23)

God never leaves, nor will forsake, he's the friend who's always near. (Prov. 18:24)
He's not a genie bottled up, uncorked so he'll appear.
If life's put first, then God is last, and his blessings will not flow.
Just let God lead; ask what he wants, and he'll show what way to go.   (Isa. 48:17)

The trick is knowing what God wants; the key is knowing him.
So we must study all God's Word, not simply scan or skim.   (2 Tim. 2:15)
We cannot pick the parts we like and toss out what we want.
It's not a menu we can browse, like in a restaurant.

God's truth is not up for debate; it shows us who he is.   (2 Tim. 3:16)
We need to serve him in all things if we choose to be his.   (Luke 8:21)
For many say they are the Lord's, yet do not follow him.   (Rom. 2:13)
When judgment comes, they may be shocked that their fate ends up grim.

God is not mocked, he won't be fooled by what we say or do.
He peers inside the heart of man; our thoughts he follows too.
You cannot be a hollow saint, no fruit can blossom there.   (1 Tim. 4:15)
If God weighed you with his scale, would you be full of air?   (Isa. 26:7)

Are you a maiden stuck outside with no oil to fill your lamp?   (Matt. 25:3)
When Jesus comes to see his bride, will your head have his stamp?   (Rev. 20:4)
If this does not make you think twice, you need to wake up now.   (Rev. 3:11)
You need to put him on the throne, you need to make this vow:

My Savior, I will put you first; I will seek out your face.   (1 Chron 16:11; Ps. 105:4)
I long to follow only you for you prepare a place.   (John 14:2)
I will choose to praise your name, to thank you in all things,   (Ps. 30:12; 1 Thess. 5:18)
To live a life that honors you no matter what life brings.   (Dan. 3:17–18)

God's Promises

The closer that I walk with God, the more he has revealed.   (Matt. 11:27)
I've seen his power in my life, his truth has been my shield.   (2 Sam. 22:3)
The Bible teaches many things; it shows me how to walk.
It taught me God is always there, my fortress and my rock.   (Ps. 18:2)

Our God has given promises to help us make it through.   (Ps. 112:1–2)
His promises bring hope to us, his promises are true.   (2 Sam. 22:31)
His promises ignite our faith and help us to stand fast.   (1 Cor. 16:13)
We serve a God who does not change, his promises will last.   (Heb. 6:17)

When we accept God's promises, we need to read them through.
We often miss a part of them, the part we need to do.
God promises to walk with us; he is our closest friend.   (Ps. 23:4)
But we must seek to do his will so blessings he can send.

His promises are like a pact, both parties must commit.
A covenant that God has made, so we must follow it.
If we declare what God has said but fail to heed his Word,
We can't be shocked when it seems like our prayers have not been heard.   (Matt. 6:7)

We cannot ask for miracles or answers to be seen
If we do not walk close to God or live a life unclean.   (Rom. 8:5, 6)
So walk with God, and then you can trust that he will meet your need.   (John 15:7)
He only asks that as his kids, his precepts we will heed.

So when you read his promises, make sure you read it all.
Missing part of what God said can make the promise stall.
He is a God who will not change; he is a righteous God,   (Dan 9:14)
And we must know what God has said, our knowledge can't be flawed.

We need to know that God wants us to live a life that's blessed.
But standing on God's promises puts our walk to the test.
God always will do as he says; God's Word says this is true.   (Ps. 71:22)
So if you do your part as well, he'll always follow through.   (Ps. 106:3)

With boldness, God wants us to come and remind him of his Word.
Our faithful God will do his part, our faith will get him stirred.
And if we walk as he would ask, our requests will be heard,
And we will see God's blessings flow; he cannot break his Word.   (Ps. 112:1–3)

Pump Up the Volume

The world today makes lots of noise with voices everywhere.
Our cars, our phones, and the internet make quiet time so rare.
Our children take the brunt of this with messages they hear.
The negative outweighs the good, it causes stress and fear. (Prov. 23:19)

More people now can criticize while you don't see their face.
They join in other people's rants while safely in their space.
The internet created this, disguised to be your friend,
It lets the wicked torment some with every text they send.

So we must be the positive to all we hear and see,
Pumping out God's truth to all in hope that some break free. (Acts 4:31)
Our kids and friends need words of hope to combat words of harm. (Ps. 7:14)
They need the truth the Bible has for lies it will disarm.

With this, they can tune out the bad, this negative barrage,
Which says the world can guide their way, and God's just a mirage.
So speak aloud for all to hear the hope our Lord can bring.
For this is how we'll light the world when darkness tries to cling. (Job 12:22)

We also need to take the time to tune out all the bad,
And make more time to sit with God, to listen to our dad.
We need to share God's healing words with people in this world,
Instead of adding to their pain when hurtful words are hurled. (Luke 6:45)

We must also walk the walk or our light grows too dim. (Deut. 26:17)
Does your walk show that Christ is Lord? It should point straight to him.
We cannot keep God to ourselves; we're in a world so lost, (John 8:26)
We need to speak with voices clear, no matter what the cost.

Our volume should be cranked up high in words and what we do.
The fruit we bear must come from God, so others want it too. (Prov. 8:19)
The fruits the Spirit gives to us are what this world has lost. (Prov. 11:30)
Love, joy, peace, kindness, and faith, these virtues have been tossed.

We cannot sit and idly wait, for he could return today.
We must arise and shout to all that Jesus is the way.   (John 14:6)
So crank it up, our time is short, and the scroll is in his hand.   (Rev. 5:5)
For angels wait, their trumpets raised, awaiting his command.   (Rev 8:6)

We can't delay saving the lost, and the time is running out.   (1 Cor. 7:29)
The world must hear that Christ is Lord, we need to sing and shout.
Like overtime, we do not know just when the game will end.
We must pump up God's Word to all, though some we will offend.   (Matt. 13:57)

If Christ returns and friends are lost, did you do all you could?
We know that all won't turn to God, we just don't know who would.
So dig down deep and stand for God, proclaim his Word out loud,
So souls escape eternal fire when every knee has bowed.   (Rom. 3:4; 14:11)

Compromise
(Psalm 119)

As I grew up, I often heard that compromise is good.
Relationships are give-and-take, a fact I understood.
But God tells me he cannot change, he will not compromise.   (Heb. 13:8)
Thinking that at times I should is one of Satan's lies.

"Just try it once," and "One time won't hurt," are phrases he could use
To make me compromise my walk and God's principles abuse.
When I give Satan a foothold, I open up a door.
Then only once is not enough, now I am craving more.

To compromise is dangerous, it is a slippery slope.
It's like I'm climbing down a wall, yet I forgot the rope.
The Bible warns that compromise can take me off God's track.
The devil knows that once I slide, it's harder to come back.

The Bible says to be diligent, but vigilant as well.
Satan uses subtle schemes, and deception he will sell.
If he can make me compromise, eventually I'll see
What started as a single sin becomes iniquity.

Remember we are in a war; our sword must be gripped tight
For every day from dawn to dusk, we're in a spiritual fight.
So stand fast to God's principles, walk close with him each day,
And when Satan tries his subtle schemes, they're quickly turned away.

The Word of God gives tips to us to resist compromise.
The truth that God has given us will combat Satan's lies.   (Ps. 119:18)
Renew our minds with truth from God, so compromise can't win,
And when we hear the whispered lies, we won't fall into sin.

Since most of us avoid conflict, compromise feels right.
Integrity, which honors God, makes people feel uptight.
When we won't do what others want, they often get upset,   (Ps. 119:22)
For they don't want to feel the guilt integrity can set.   (Ps. 119:31)

Remember that integrity is how we honor God.

Compromising what he asks makes us become a fraud.   (Ps. 119:29)

Ask God to help, as David did, please don't give up on me,   (Ps. 119:8)

So you can live a joyful life, full of integrity.   (Ps. 119:1, 35)

His Word tells me to seek the Lord, search hard with all my heart.   (Ps. 119:2, 10)

Then hide his Word deep in my heart, so his ways won't depart.   (Ps. 110:11)

For God's Word is my only hope, so I don't compromise.   (Ps. 119:49)

Then when life knocks me to the ground, his promise helps me rise.   (Ps. 119:50)

For your Word, Lord, is in my heart, it makes my soul rejoice.

It flows out from my hand as ink; my poem is my voice.

I thank you, God, for two full years that you have filled my heart,

And let me write these odes of love that never will depart.

I know I still have lots to learn, but you have given me

The hope to battle compromise with your Word as the key.

I pray that you still speak to me in whispers and in verse,

So I can glorify your name with poems you disperse.

I do not know what you've planned next, but give me the strength to seek.

And speak to me in whole or part, I only need a peek.

I praise your name for all you've done, the courage you've instilled.

I want to serve you every day, so please let my soul be filled.

(Thank you, Lord, for this two-year journey. Thank you for allowing me the honor to share the words you have given me. You are the author, the beginning, and the finisher of my faith. Thank you for choosing me!)

Printed in the United States
by Baker & Taylor Publisher Services